IT FOR THE
99%

The Small Business Owner's "IT Hat" Guide

BRADY HELKENN

ISBN: 978-1-7340909-1-8 (paperback)
ISBN: 978-1-7340909-2-5 (e-book)

Copyediting, design, and production by Backspace Ink

Graphics by Vecteezy.com

A Word of Thanks + A Word About Niko

Before we begin, I want to take a moment to thank a rising star in the cybersecurity world: Niko Nikolaidis, who is formally joining this book as a contributing author. Niko helped sharpen the thinking behind several chapters through multiple drafts of this book and contributed Chapter 5. "NIST Standards: What, Why, and How to Implement Them" as his own original work, written in his own voice. His deep focus on cybersecurity, combined with a fresh, next-generation lens, made him a natural fit for this book, and I'm grateful to have his expertise included here.

Contents

Foreword 13

Introduction..15
What This Book Is (and What It's Not)...............................15
Why I Wrote This Book..16
How to Use This Book..16

List of Acronyms and Abbreviations............................19

Glossary: Key Terms and Concepts 21

PART I. THE FOUNDATION..27

Chapter 1. The IT Mindset Shift....................................29
Start Thinking Like a Leader..29
The "Just Make It Work" Trap..30
Small Business, Big Targets 30
You Don't Need to Be an IT Expert. But You Do Need a System.............31
Budgets for IT: A Necessity, NOT a Luxury 32
Case Stories: The REAL Cost of Doing Nothing 33
The TL;DR...35

Chapter 2. Centralization (and Consolidation) Are Critical 37

What Is Tool Sprawl? 37

Why Scattered Tools Kill Your Scalability 38

Choose Your Home Base: Google Workspace or Microsoft 365 41

Why Centralized, Admin-Controlled Accounts Matter 43

Shadow IT: The Invisible Threat 44

Centralized Control vs. Shadow IT..45

Why GoDaddy (or Personal Gmails) for Your Business Email
    Is a Terrible Idea 46

Commit to One Storage System (Google Drive vs. SharePoint
    vs. Box) ... and NOT Dropbox 48

File Storage Platform Comparison 50

Case Stories: When Too Many Tools Become the Problem 51

The TL;DR... 53

Chapter 3. Back Up Before You Blackout................................. 55

Cloud Storage Is Not a Backup 55

The "Oh, !@#$" Moment Every Business Eventually Has.......................56

What Real Backup Looks Like..56

Why We Love (and Use) Spanning 57

Why Dropbox Is Not a Backup Tool... 57

Layer Your Backup Strategy 58

The Three Tiers of Backup 59

The 3-2-1 Backup Rule...59

Case Stories: What Happens When You Don't Have a Plan........................60

The TL;DR...61

Chapter 4. Cyber Liability Insurance: Your Financial Firewall 63

What Happens If You Get Hit? 63

Why General Liability Isn't Enough 63
What Cyber Insurance Actually Covers 64
Why It Matters What Cyber Liability Insurance Actually Covers 66
How to Shop for a Policy without Getting Screwed 67
Why It (and IT) Should Be in Your Budget EVERY Year 69
What Your Cyber Policy *Should* Include...70
My Broker Said I'm Covered. Am I?...71
How to Get Denied (and Not Even Know It).....................................72
Case Stories: Cyber Liability Insurance in the Real World................73
The TL;DR...74

PART II. SECURITY, CONTROL, AND DIGITAL HYGIENE 77

Chapter 5. NIST Standards: What, Why, and How to Implement Them 79

The Mentality of NIST 79
What Is NIST?...80
Why NIST Matters for Small Businesses..80
The NIST Cybersecurity Framework.. 81
Step-by-Step Application.. 81
What About NIST SP 800-171? 84
A Basic NIST-Based Small Business Security List.............................84
Final Thoughts: Start Small, Scale Securely 85

Chapter 6. Security That Scales 87

Security Mindset 87
Start with MFA...87
With and Without MFA..88
What "Remember This Device" Does 89

Your Antivirus Software Is Not Enough Anymore 91

Email Is Still the #1 Attack Vector.. 92

Passwords Are a Team Sport.. 94

Security Is a Culture, Not a Checkbox... 95

Case Stories: When Security Scales, So Does Confidence 96

The TL;DR.. 98

Chapter 7. User Access and Risk Management 99

Rethinking Access 99

Common-Sense Access: Trust with Boundaries 100

Shared Logins Are a Security Nightmare.. 101

Offboarding Is Where Most Breaches Begin 101

Temporary Access Should Be ... Temporary 102

Shared Drives and Shared Sites Done Right 102

You Can't Protect What You Don't Know You Have.................................... 103

Case Stories: Access Control Done Right (and Wrong)............................. 104

The TL;DR.. 105

Chapter 8. Build Workflows That Scale with You 107

Why Workflow Matters 107

Let Your Process Define Your Tools... 108

The Power of Consistent Folder Structures and Naming 108

Templates Are a Secret Weapon 109

Don't Reinvent the Wheel — Steal from Yourself...................................... 109

Automate the Busywork with Intentionality... 110

Document Your Process Now, Not Later... 111

Automate First, Delegate Second, Do Last 111

Case Stories: Simplicity, Naming, and Workflow That Works 113

The TL;DR.. 115

PART III. TOOLS THAT WORK FOR YOU (NOT AGAINST YOU) 117

Chapter 9. SaaS That Works for the 1-20 Crowd................. 119
SaaS for the 99%...119
What "Best in Class" Really Means at Your Size 120
Core Categories to Get Right... 120
Integrations Are a Superpower 122
Beware of Custom Apps... 123
Don't Buy a Tool for Just One Client..................................... 123
Case Stories: Choosing SaaS Tools That Actually Work 124
The TL;DR 125

Chapter 10. Plan for the Worst (So You Can Stay at Your Best)..... 127
Not If, But When 127
Disaster Recovery vs. Business Continuity: What's the Difference? 128
Start with These Questions 128
Create a "Business Down" Checklist 129
Write It Down — But It Matters More to Test 130
When to Involve Your IT Provider 130
Case Stories: Business Continuity in Real Life 131
The TL;DR 133

PART IV. GROWTH BUILDING...135

Chapter 11. Your Machines Age: Know How to Budget and When to Upgrade 137
Why Hardware Still Matters in a Cloud-Centric World....................137
BYOD vs. Company-Owned: Choose Your Adventure (Wisely)............ 138
The Silent Budget Killer: Random, Reactive Buying............... 139

Get Organized Before You Buy Anything 140

Depreciation and Lifecycle: Plan for the Inevitable 141

Budget Like a Grown-Up Business 142

Warranties, Support, and Vendor Selection 142

Refurbs, Hand-Me-Downs, and the Right Way to Recycle.......143

Case Stories: Surprise Costs vs. Budgeted Spend 144

The TL;DR..145

Chapter 12. When (and How) to Outsource IT the Smart Way 147

Recognizing When You Need Help 147

The IT Outsourcing Continuum 148

The Signs It's Time to Outsource IT 151

Questions to Ask an IT Partner Before You Sign Anything.....152

Red Flags to Watch Out For...153

Don't Abdicate — Delegate..154

Audit Your IT Provider: Trust. But Verify 155

Why "Too Small" Is a Myth..157

Case Stories: Smart IT Outsourcing in Action............................158

The TL;DR...160

Chapter 13. The IT Growth Plan: From 1 to 20 and Beyond 161

Growth Needs to Be Intentional 161

Stage 1. Solo Doesn't Mean Sloppy...162

Stage 2. The First Hires: Structure Before You Scale................162

Stage 3. 5–10 People: Time to Get Proactive 167

Stage 4. 10–20+ People: IT as a Strategic Lever........................168

Growth Without Burnout: Build Before You Break 169

Case Stories: IT That Grows with You..169

The TL;DR...170

Chapter 14. Remote Work Done Right:
IT for Distributed Teams 173

Most Small Businesses Are Remote Now 173

Why Remote Teams Need a Different IT Discipline 173

Essential Remote Infrastructure...174

Device Management Basics (Even for Small Teams) 175

Remote Onboarding and Offboarding Checklist................. 176

Build Your Remote Culture around Security........................177

Lesson Learned...177

The TL;DR... 178

PART V. LESSONS FROM THE TRENCHES 179

Chapter 15. Where HR Meets IT: Security, Monitoring,
and Onboarding... 181

Why HR and IT Are More Intertwined Than Ever.................181

Background Checks and Prehire Risk Screening................. 182

Onboarding: The First Security Policy Your Employee Signs 183

Monitoring: What's Legal, What's Practical, What's Ethical...................184

Termination Protocols... 187

Case Stories: Due Diligence in HR and When It Fails 188

The TL;DR..190

Chapter 16. Regulated But Resilient: IT for Compliance-Heavy
Industries...193

Compliance-First Attitude 193

Key Regulatory Frameworks Small Businesses Encounter.....................194

Documentation and Data Retention 195

IT Practices That Support Compliance 197

CONTENTS

Choose the Right Tools and Vendors 199

What Auditors and Examiners Look For..199

Case Stories: Regulatory Scares and Close Calls.........................201

The TL;DR.. 202

Chapter 17. Bonus Case Studies: What It Looks Like in the Wild .. 205

Why IT Matters 205

What a Ransomware Attack Feels Like.. 205

Case Stories: Successful Outcomes 206

The TL;DR.. 208

Chapter 18. You're Not Alone: Next Steps and Support 211

What's Next? 211

Step 1: Do a Quick IT Self-Check 212

Step 2. Pick One Area to Improve 212

Step 3. Build or Find Your Support System 212

This Book Is Just the Beginning... 213

The TL;DR.. 213

Appendix A. References List 215

Appendix B. Starter Kit and Core Stack Guide 221

The Core Stack (Essentials for Every Size Business)........................ 221

Tools by Industry..224

Tools by Company Size..225

Setup Priorities 226

Appendix C: Resources.. 227

Free Resources.. 227

Stay Current: Key Regulatory Resources...................................... 227

Foreword

I first met Brady in 2000 when we were doing IT for a mid-sized San Francisco civil engineering firm. At the time, Brady — along with the IT Director and a couple of other team members — was responsible for all end-user and systems support for a 120+ employee, multilocation and multiserver, live production CAD and engineering environment. The company worked on many time-sensitive projects for Tier-1 facilities, hospitals, and police stations, and had one of the leading HVAC design practices for Tier 3 and Tier 4 data centers.

The users and environment needed to be ALWAYS-ON, and data integrity and availability were paramount to the business. Brady was instrumental in achieving these goals, but when the confines of the corporate IT team got to be too much for him, he went out and started his own practice. He subsequently grew that practice to an impressive scale, often setting trends in our industry by addressing segments of the market that others were afraid to touch — or hadn't found success in — particularly servicing micro businesses and those with fewer than 10 employees.

Brady figuratively — and now literally — wrote the book on providing managed IT and security services for this segment of the market. With this book, he has written a comprehensive technology compendium that should accompany every small business operator as they scale their business. This book will not only help the operator reduce risk along the way but ensure they get the most out of their technology investments; it's an A to Z how-to for producing a technology ecosystem that delivers on business outcomes.

It's not just some high-level overview. It's a step-by-step guide, grounded in real-world experience, that speaks the language of the small business owner and empowers them to lead with confidence.

—Alex Rayter

Introduction

Let's be honest. Most books about IT are written for IT people. This one isn't.

This book is for the solo consultants, the boutique agencies, the multihat managers, and the small and agile teams who don't have the time — or desire — to become tech experts but know they can't afford to ignore it anymore. Whether you're a therapist, coach, law firm partner, creative agency founder, or financial planner, this book is for you.

More broadly, this book is for anyone who's ever googled "how to secure my business email" at midnight after hearing about a phishing attack. It's also for anyone who's ever had that sinking feeling when something stopped working and realized, "I have no backup plan."

What This Book Is (and What It's Not)

This is not a technical manual. There are no step-by-step tutorials or deep-dive certifications here.

What you will find is a practical, conversational guide to IT, written like a one-on-one Zoom call with someone who's been in the trenches for over a decade, helping businesses like yours untangle their IT infrastructure, secure their systems, and build an IT foundation that actually scales with them.

The goal isn't to turn you into an IT consultant. It's to help you think like a business leader who understands the cost of downtime, the value of systems, and the return on investment of getting your infrastructure right the first time.

Why I Wrote This Book

After years of working with small businesses — and watching some of them grow while others crumbled under the weight of their own tech chaos — I saw the same patterns.

They weren't failing because they didn't care. They were failing because no one had ever explained IT in a way that *made sense to them*. Most advice was either too vague or too technical, written for corporations or techies—never for that scrappy, smart business owner juggling 10 things at once.

This book is my attempt to fill that gap.

It's also personal. I've seen firsthand what happens when people assume that "just make it work" is enough — until it doesn't. And I've also seen the relief, confidence, and growth that come from getting it right, often with just a few small but strategic shifts.

I've seen small businesses fail too often. This isn't a corporation you're losing; most of the time, it's your livelihood. And if this book can reach someone before it's too late, *that's* my ultimate goal.

How to Use This Book

I encourage you to read this book front to back your first time through. The chapters build on each other — from mindset and structure to security and scalability. But, after that, think of this book as your IT reference manual. Bookmark it. Highlight it. Come back to it any time you're stuck, planning for growth, or facing a new decision about your tools, vendors, or systems.

Not every chapter will apply equally to everyone, and that's okay. If you're solo, some of the team-scaling material may not be relevant *yet*. If you're in a compliance-heavy industry, you may want to jump ahead to Part V. "Lessons from the Trenches." This book is built to flex with your business.

Let's get started! First up: a "List of Acronyms and Abbreviations" used in this book.

List of Acronyms and Abbreviations

2FA.................... two-factor authentication

ADHD .... attention-deficit/hyperactivity disorder

API .... application programming interface

BAA .... business associate agreement

BYOD .... bring your own device

CAD.................. computer-aided design

CIO .... chief information officer

CRM.................. customer/client relationship manager

CSF .... [NIST] Cybersecurity Framework

CUI................... Controlled Unclassified Information

DIY.................... do it yourself

DLP................... data loss prevention

DRP.................. disaster recovery plan

E&O.................. errors and omissions

EA .... executive assistant

EDR................... endpoint detection and response

FINRA.............. Financial Industry Regulatory Authority

GDPR................ General Data Protection Regulation

HDD .... hard disk drive

HIPAA .... Health Insurance Portability and Accountability Act

HR..................... human resources

IP...................... intellectual property

IT...................... information technology

MDM................. mobile device management

MFA .... multi-factor authentication

MSP .... managed service provider

MSSP............... managed security service provider

NAS .... network-attached storage

NIST .... National Institute of Standards and Technology

NVMe.............. Non-Volatile Memory Express

PHI.................... protected healthcare information

PII...................... personally identifying information

RMM .... remote monitoring and management

SaaS .... Software as a Service

SEC................... Securities and Exchange Commission

SEO .... search engine optimization

SIEM .... security information and event management

SLA................... service level agreement

SMB.................. small- and medium-sized business

SOC 2............... System and Organization Controls 2

SSD................... solid-state drive

TL;DR................ too long; didn't read

UI .... user interface

VA .... virtual assistant

vCIO................. virtual chief information officer

VPN .... virtual private network

Wi-Fi................. wireless fidelity

WORM .... write once, read many

Glossary: Key Terms and Concepts

2FA or 2-Step Verification: See MFA.

Access creep: When employees accumulate unnecessary system access over time, increasing the risk of accidental or malicious data exposure.

Admin-controlled account: An account created and managed by the business rather than by the employee. Crucial for secure onboarding/offboarding.

API: A set of rules and tools that allows different software applications to communicate with each other, enabling data sharing, feature integration, and automation between systems.

Audit trail: A secure record of who accessed what data, when, and how. Useful for both security and compliance.

BAA: A legally required contract under HIPAA between a healthcare provider (or related business) and any third-party vendor that handles PHI. It ensures the vendor agrees to safeguard the data according to HIPAA standards.

Backup: A duplicate copy of your data stored separately to protect against loss. Often includes automated, cloud-based solutions.

Brute-force attack: A type of hacking attempt where a person or automated tool attempts to repeatedly guess username/password combinations to get into specific user accounts, such as global administrator accounts. It relies on volume, not subtlety.

Business continuity: A plan to keep operations running during emergencies, including IT, communications, and staffing procedures.

BYOD: Commonly used in HR and IT circles to describe the use of a contractor or employee's use of a personal computer and/or mobile device for business activities.

Cloud storage: A way to store files online so they can be accessed from anywhere. (Important distinction: Cloud storage is not the same as a backup. True backup solutions include version history, restore points, and automation for disaster recovery.)

Compliance: Adhering to industry regulations (like HIPAA or FINRA) that govern data security, privacy, and IT operations.

CRM: A SaaS tool like HubSpot or Salesforce used to track, organize, and manage communications with prospects and clients throughout the sales process. It's a major upgrade from spreadsheets and essential when multiple salespeople need shared access to lead and customer data.

Disaster recovery: A component of business continuity focused on restoring IT systems, data, and operations after a major disruption (ransomware, fire, hardware failure). This includes predefined steps, roles, and technologies for getting back online quickly and securely. Often formalized in a DRP.

DLP: A set of tools and policies designed to detect and prevent unauthorized access, sharing, or leakage of sensitive data — whether accidentally or maliciously — across email, cloud storage, and endpoint devices.

DRP: A documented strategy outlining how a business will restore IT operations and data after a disruptive event. Often a formalized component of a broader business continuity plan.

E&O: A type of professional liability insurance that protects businesses and individuals against claims of negligence, mistakes, or failure to deliver services as promised. Common in fields like IT, law, finance, and consulting.

EDR: A cybersecurity solution that monitors devices (endpoints) for suspicious activity, enables real-time threat detection, and allows remote response actions like isolating or wiping a compromised machine. EDR goes beyond antivirus software by focusing on behavior, not just known threats.

Endpoint security: Protection for devices like laptops, desktops, and phones against malware, phishing, or unauthorized access.

FINRA: A US nonprofit organization that regulates broker-dealers and securities firms to protect investors and ensure market integrity through rules enforcement, licensing, and oversight.

GDPR: A European Union law that governs how personal data is collected, used, and stored, giving individuals more control over their information and requiring organizations to follow strict privacy and security standards.

HDD: An older hard-drive technology that uses magnetic spinning disks to read from and write to the hard drive.

HIPAA: A US law that sets national standards for protecting sensitive patient health information, requiring healthcare providers and their business associates to implement safeguards for privacy, security, and data breach notification.

IP ownership: The legal right to control and profit from creative work, inventions, or proprietary assets such as logos, code, content, and business processes. IP ownership should be clearly defined in privacy and other HR policies to ensure the company retains rights to what's created.

IT: The use of computers, software, networks, and systems to store, process, transmit, and manage data for business operations and communication.

Least privilege: A security principle that gives users the minimum access necessary to perform their job.

MDM: A system for centrally managing company-owned laptops, tablets, and smartphones. MDM allows IT to enforce security settings, remotely wipe lost devices, and ensure compliance. Unlike RMM, MDM focuses specifically on mobile and portable endpoints.

MFA (also known as **2FA or 2-Step Verification**): A security method requiring two or more forms of verification before granting access. This could be a password + a mobile app code, fingerprint, or physical token.

MSP: A third-party company that remotely manages a business' IT infrastructure and end-user systems, typically on a subscription or contract basis.

MSSP: A specialized third-party company that monitors, manages, and responds to cybersecurity threats for businesses, often providing services like firewall management, threat detection, and incident response on a subscription basis.

NAS: A centralized device for storing and sharing files on a local network. NAS is often used when cloud storage or full file servers aren't ideal. But it may lack robust backup features and typically requires a VPN for remote access.

NVMe: A high-speed storage protocol designed for SSDs, considered a more modern version than SATA (its predecessor)

PHI / PII: Often referenced by regulatory bodies as a type of data subject to privacy and security requirements. These are often the most valuable targets from a hacker's perspective.

Phishing: A type of cyberattack where hackers trick users into giving up credentials or downloading malware, usually via email.

Retention policy: A rule about how long data (especially emails, files, or backups) must be kept for legal or business reasons.

RMM: A tool typically used by MSPs to monitor, manage, and patch systems remotely, including servers, workstations, and networks. RMM offers broader control than MDM, often including scripting, automation, and alerting capabilities.

SaaS: Cloud-based software that you subscribe to (instead of installing locally) (Google Workspace, Microsoft 365).

SEC: A US government agency that enforces federal securities laws, regulates financial markets, and protects investors by overseeing securities exchanges, brokers, and public companies.

Shadow IT: Any tech or software employees use without IT's knowledge or approval, often creating security and compliance risks.

SOC 2: A cybersecurity compliance standard that evaluates how well a service provider manages customer data based on five trust principles: security, availability, processing integrity, confidentiality, and privacy. Commonly required for SaaS and cloud service vendors.

Social engineering: A type of cyberattack that uses deception — often through emails, calls, or messages — to manipulate people into giving up sensitive information, system access, or money. It targets human trust rather than technical vulnerabilities.

SSD: A fast, reliable data storage device with no moving parts, using flash memory to store information. Offers quicker boot times, faster file access, and better durability compared to traditional HDDs.

TL;DR: An internet shorthand used to introduce a brief summary of a longer text or to signal a condensed explanation.

UI: The visual and interactive elements of a software application or device that allow users to interact with it, including buttons, menus, icons, and layout design. A well-designed UI makes technology easier and more intuitive to use.

vCIO: An outsourced IT advisor who helps small businesses plan and align their technology strategy with business goals without the cost of a full-time executive. Often provided by MSPs as part of ongoing services.

VPN: A secure, encrypted connection that allows users to access a private network (like a company's internal systems) over the internet. It's commonly used by remote workers to safely connect to file servers, NAS devices, or on-prem apps. VPNs are also used by individuals (via services like NordVPN or ExpressVPN) to protect their internet privacy, mask their IP address, and encrypt their online activity, especially when using public Wi-Fi or browsing from countries with restricted internet access.

Wi-Fi: A wireless technology that allows devices to connect to the internet or a local network using radio waves, often eliminating the need for physical cables.

WORM: A type of data storage required by FINRA/SEC regulations that prevents alteration or deletion once data is written. It ensures records (emails, financial documents) are preserved in a tamper-proof format for regulatory compliance.

PART I

The Foundation

CHAPTER 1

The IT Mindset Shift

Start Thinking Like a Leader

First up: the mindset shift that separates accidental tech chaos from intentional IT strategy.

Let's be real. Most small business owners don't wake up excited about IT. You didn't start your law firm, coaching business, or financial consultancy because you love configuring email security settings. You did it because you're good at what you do. But here's the truth no one tells you until it's too late: **Tech isn't just the thing that powers your business. It's the thing that can bring it to its knees if you don't take it seriously.**

With over 78% of U.S. small- and midsized businesses already leveraging cloud services,[1] the question isn't *if* you should modernize your IT, it's whether you're doing it smartly, securely, and cost-effectively.

Now, before you run for the hills, I promise that this book is not here to turn you into an IT person or *make you paranoid*. You don't need to know how to write code, set up a server, or even understand what half the jargon means. You just need to start **thinking like the leader of a business that runs on technology** because you are.

The "Just Make It Work" Trap

I've worked with hundreds of freelancers and small businesses, and one pattern shows up again and again. It goes like this:

- You start with your personal email account because it's easy.
- You grab a free trial of whatever software looks helpful that week.
- You hand off access to a virtual assistant without changing security settings.
- You back up files by ... well, not really backing them up.

And for a while, it works — until one day, it doesn't. Your email gets hacked. A client's confidential data goes missing. A laptop is stolen, and you can't remember who had access to what. Suddenly, you're in damage-control mode, and what started as "just make it work" becomes "how did we get here?"

Small Business, Big Targets

There's a myth that hackers only go after the big guys like Fortune 500 companies, hospitals, and major retailers. In reality, small businesses are low-hanging fruit. Not because they're being directly *targeted* in a James-Bond-villain kind of way but because they're caught in massive, automated attacks. Think of it like a fishing trawler: The hackers cast a wide net (email lists, IP scans, exploit kits) and your business, though small, gets scooped up along with everyone else.

They don't need to know your name to steal your data or lock you out of your systems.

Why does this work so often?

♦ You probably don't have an IT department.

♦ Your security tools are likely outdated or nonexistent.

♦ You may not even know what you're supposed to be protecting.

And the stakes are brutal. A single cyberattack could shut down your operations, cost you thousands in lost revenue, and permanently damage your reputation. But, in addition to the costs mentioned, nearly two-thirds of small businesses completely fail and shut down in the months following a successful data breach or ransomware attack.[2]

Not budgeting for IT doesn't save you time or money — it borrows against your future. As I've stated many times, a good infrastructure is like a bulletproof vest: It doesn't do you any good to wait until after you get shot to use it.

You Don't Need to Be an IT Expert. But You Do Need a System

The goal here isn't to overwhelm you with tech. It's to give you a **framework** — a way to think about your IT setup that grows with your business. Whether you're a one-person shop or running a 15-person team, you need to understand:

♦ What systems run your business

♦ Who has access to these systems

♦ How data is protected and backed up

♦ What happens if something goes wrong

Think of it like managing your finances. You don't need to be an accountant. But you'd never hand your credit card to a stranger and say, "Do whatever." Tech is no different.

Remember: Downtime isn't just annoying — it's expensive. For small businesses, the cost of IT downtime can range from $137 to $427 per minute.[3] That's why foundational IT choices like backups, hardware, and networking aren't just technical details. They're financial decisions.

Working with an IT company can absolutely help you build this framework and, in many cases, you'll want to delegate the day-to-day administration to them. But you still need to understand the big picture because handing it off completely and hoping for the best is how businesses end up locked out of their own systems. Leadership doesn't mean doing it all yourself — it means staying informed and steering the ship.

Budgets for IT: A Necessity, NOT a Luxury

Here's the part many small businesses miss: IT is not just a cost. It's a line item that protects everything else you spend money on.

◆ Your staff can't work if the systems are down.

◆ Your client data is worthless (and dangerous) if it's leaked.

◆ Your reputation can't survive a sloppy data breach.

So, whether it's $500/month for secure backups or $20,000/year for professional help, you're not throwing money into the void. You're investing in your uptime, your privacy, and your peace of mind.

RULE OF THUMB

Budget between **$300 to $500 per month per person** for IT. (Depending on your business structure, "person" may be an employee or a contractor, full time or part time.) That includes everything from licenses and backups to support, security tools, and even hardware like laptops, workstations, and networking equipment. It may sound like a lot. But when you consider what's at stake — and how technology powers nearly every part of your business — it's one of the smartest investments you can make. •

Case Stories: The REAL Cost of Doing Nothing

The following stories reflect two sides of the same coin: one business that ignored IT risks until it was too late and another that got ahead of the curve just in time. Both reinforce the idea that modern businesses — regardless of size — live and die by their IT infrastructure.

Engineering Firm: The Cost of Complacency

Background: A nine-person civil engineering firm had been using a mix of personal Gmail accounts, Dropbox, and legacy CAD software without centralized IT oversight. Their "IT plan" was to rely on a break/fix IT consultant who charged by the hour and only showed up when something was broken. Most issues were patched reactively, and anything beyond the basics — like email security or backups — was never discussed.

The Problem: One employee opened a phishing email that led to a credential breach. Without MFA or a centralized email platform, the attacker sat quietly in the compromised inbox, monitoring communications for weeks. Eventually, a fraudulent invoice was sent to a client who paid it.

The Fix: The client alerted the firm. But, by then, the attacker had already vanished. The engineering firm lost the client and over $18,000, and their reputation took a major hit. They brought in an IT company only after the breach to rebuild.

The Outcome: Months of cleanup, a full rebranding effort, and a painful reminder that "doing nothing" costs far more than being proactive.

Lesson Learned: If you're exchanging sensitive files, contracts, or plans with clients, you need real infrastructure. Waiting until you're attacked is like buying a fire extinguisher after a fire erupts.

Solo Attorney: Big Moves, Small Team

Background: A solo attorney with a growing caseload was tired of tech issues getting in the way of her work. She had heard too many horror stories from colleagues who'd lost cases — or clients — due to IT failures. She decided to get ahead of it.

The Problem: Her setup was cobbled together: Gmail, a personal Dropbox, a free Zoom account, and no real backup strategy. She knew it wasn't sustainable.

The Fix: She signed up with a boutique IT provider who migrated her to Google Workspace, set up a secure password manager, automated cloud backups, and added IRONSCALES for phishing protection.

The Outcome: When a phishing attempt hit her inbox weeks later, IRONSCALES caught it. She reported it, triggering a scan across other client inboxes. Nothing got through. No damage. Just a quick, confident email to her IT vendor: "Handled."

Lesson Learned: Small businesses that act like big businesses protect themselves like big businesses. Size doesn't matter — systems
do.

The TL;DR

- You don't have to become an IT nerd. But you *do* need to start
  thinking like a business leader who values infrastructure.

- Small businesses are juicy targets for cybercriminals because
  they're usually underprotected.

- A sloppy IT setup might work — for a while. But, when it breaks,
  it *really* breaks.

- Budgeting for IT is like buying insurance for your operations.
  It's what keeps the lights on when things go sideways.

You've seen why IT can't be treated as an afterthought. Now it's time
to tackle one of the most common sources of small-business tech
chaos: scattered tools and siloed systems. In the next chapter, we'll
show you why centralization isn't about control. It's about clarity,
security, and scalability.

Up next, we'll dig into the first major shift: **centralizing your tools
and accounts**, so you stop playing tech Jenga and start building a
solid foundation.

CHAPTER 2

Centralization (and Consolidation) Are Critical

What Is Tool Sprawl?

Let's play a game called "Spot the IT Dumpster Fire":

- Your email is on GoDaddy or you're using a free Gmail or Hotmail account.
- Your documents are split between Dropbox, Box, and someone's desktop folder.
- You use Gmail for one project and Outlook for another.
- No one knows who set up the calendar ... or how to fix it.

Sound familiar?

This kind of tool sprawl is the norm for small businesses. And, when it's just you, you can *kind of* get away with duct-taping your tech stack together. But if you ever plan to hire someone — even a virtual assistant — this chaos becomes a problem fast.

And on the note of the importance of your email? It's your most targeted attack surface. In fact, over 90% of successful cyberattacks begin with a phishing email.[4] That's why treating business email with the seriousness it deserves is nonnegotiable.

Why Scattered Tools Kill Your Scalability

Every new tool you bolt on without a plan creates more to manage:

- More logins to track
- More subscriptions to forget about
- More data silos that don't talk to each other
- More tools for hackers to potentially breach
- More risk when someone leaves and still has access

Think of your IT like a kitchen. If your plates are in the hallway, the cups are in the garage, and the forks are in your sock drawer, you're going to waste a lot of time making lunch. Centralizing means putting all your tools where they belong — under one roof where you (and your future team) can find them, secure them, and manage them.

Real-World Example: Too Many Tools, Not Enough Control

This small law firm had just six people, and it looked like they had things "kind of" working. But under the hood? It was a spaghetti mess:

- Microsoft 365 was set up through GoDaddy, which limited admin control.
- Personal Gmail accounts were being used for Google Calendar (for some employees only).
- Dropbox was used for file sharing. But it was all under a *single shared login* with no user-based permissions.

- Some clients required Box, so they used that too — but only for those clients.

- For passwords, it was the Wild West: One person used LastPass, another used Dashlane, and the others just remembered everything (or didn't).

On the surface, it seemed like they were saving money by cobbling tools together. In reality, they were bleeding time, exposing themselves to security risks, and completely sabotaging their ability to scale.

When they finally decided to clean it all up, the migration pain was real:

- **Consolidating passwords:** Moving the team to a single password manager took time and patience. People had to learn a new workflow, and it wasn't smooth at first. But, once trained, the risk dropped dramatically, and password-related issues dropped significantly.

- **Leaving GoDaddy's Microsoft 365:** We had to migrate their email and data into a clean, independent Microsoft 365 tenant to regain full admin rights and access to the full feature set.

- **Switching to Google Workspace:** Since they were half-using Google Calendar anyway, they made the full switch by moving from Microsoft 365 to Google Workspace. (We couldn't do this until they were out from under GoDaddy's thumb.) This allowed centralized calendars, shared drives, and cleaner collaboration. It also meant training staff to stop using Outlook.

- **Switching from Dropbox to Box:** We migrated all files out of Dropbox and consolidated everything into Box, which offered better permission control, compliance capabilities, and a more business-friendly admin interface. Since this was something a few clients already required, this allowed them to pick one storage solution and make it consistent for all their data.

♦ **Gmail vs. Outlook:** This migration required the most coaching. People had to learn a new interface, and old habits die hard. But having everything under one roof finally made IT management and support straightforward, and Outlook-related problems disappeared entirely.

It took a few months, and a lot of resistance early on. But now they're organized, secure, and scalable. And nobody misses the chaos.

Before vs. After: Chaos to Clarity

Email

♦ Before (scattered chaos): Microsoft 365 (via GoDaddy)

♦ After (centralized and scalable): Google Workspace (business-managed)

Calendars

♦ Before (scattered chaos): Mix of personal Gmail + Outlook

♦ After (centralized and scalable): Unified Google Calendar

File storage

♦ Before (scattered chaos): Dropbox (shared login), Box (for select clients)

♦ After (centralized and scalable): Consolidated into Box with proper user permissions

Passwords

♦ Before (scattered chaos): Mix of LastPass, Dashlane, and memory-only

- After (centralized and scalable): One centralized password manager for all staff

Admin control

- Before (scattered chaos): No global visibility or control
- After (centralized and scalable): Full control through Google Workspace admin console

This information helped the business see what they *were* living with — and how much smoother life could be when everything worked together.

Choose Your Home Base: Google Workspace or Microsoft 365

Choosing between Google Workspace and Microsoft 365 isn't about which one is "better." They both have their own pros and cons. It's about which one fits *you*. Most businesses don't pick intentionally. They stumble into one, then pay the price later when it doesn't scale or support their workflow.

Here's a quick way to think about it:

Quick Decision Guide

If you answer "yes" to any of these questions, lean toward Microsoft 365:

- Is Outlook already heavily used by you or your staff?
- Do you rely on advanced Excel features like Power Query or Macros?
- Do you need HIPAA/FINRA compliance tools with more granular control?

If you answer "yes" to any of these questions, lean toward Google Workspace:

♦ Do you love Gmail and Google Calendar and already use them daily?

♦ Is real-time collaboration in Docs or Sheets crucial to your workflow?

♦ Do you want to simplify onboarding with minimal training?

♦ Are you using Chromebooks or Mac-only environments?

Real-World Example: The Outlook-Heavy Finance Firm

A seven-person financial planning group chose Microsoft 365 because three senior partners *lived* in Outlook and Excel. They were also dealing with a mixed environment: Some staff used Windows machines and others used Macs, which created inconsistent behavior in Outlook and other Office apps.

As part of the transition, we standardized the entire team on business-grade Windows laptops, which gave them a more consistent support experience and eliminated weird sync bugs and file-compatibility issues.

We paired Microsoft 365 with Redtail CRM and Spanning for backups. It wasn't trendy — especially for staff who were used to their Macs — but it was practical, stable, and easy to manage going forward. And they were ultimately much happier for it.

Real-World Example: The Remote Coaching Team

A virtual coaching firm with 12 coaches around the country went with Google Workspace. Why? They needed real-time collaboration on course materials and quick file sharing, and they didn't want to deal with Outlook. Bonus points? It allowed for seamless calendar booking, fast setup, and minimal training.

Hybrid Environments Are a Trap

Some businesses try to straddle both Microsoft 365 and Google Workspace platforms. For example, they run Microsoft 365 but rely on Google Calendar. Or they edit Google Docs but use Outlook for email. That seems flexible, but it creates chaos in practice:

- Passwords and access control become harder.
- Data becomes fragmented.
- Admin rights are split or lost entirely.
- IT vendors have a harder time successfully supporting either environment.
- New hires will be much more confused and struggle to adopt your systems properly when there isn't enough consistency.

If you're considering a hybrid setup, talk to an IT professional first. You'll need tight rules, technical skills, and clear priorities to pull it off. *And, even then,* it often causes more friction than flexibility.

Why Centralized, Admin-Controlled Accounts Matter

One of the most critical — yet most overlooked — pillars of a scalable IT system is **centralized control**. If your company's email, files, and tools are spread across personal Gmail accounts, consumer Dropbox folders, or software nobody even knew your team was using, you're playing with fire ... and it has very little to do with trust in your staff.

Here's why admin control matters:

- **You can reset a password if someone leaves.** If a staff member used their personal Gmail to run client communications and they quit (or worse, were terminated), you have *no legal or technical access* to that data. Even in cases of *absolute trust*, you still can't take over that account as easily as you could in a centralized environment.

♦ **You can't get support without it.** Most SaaS platforms will only assist someone with verified admin credentials (not to mention that many don't even have support for free products at all!). If everything's tied to random personal accounts, you're locked out when it matters most.

♦ **You can see who has access to what.** With proper admin privileges, you can audit who's touching sensitive data, what they're accessing, and when. Without that visibility, it's anyone's guess. Again, this doesn't have to do with trust in your team. How can you validate proper security controls in order to qualify for cyber liability coverage or give your own clients peace of mind?

Shadow IT: The Invisible Threat

"Shadow IT" refers to tools, apps, or systems that employees use outside of company oversight without approval, visibility, or integration into your core systems. Think: someone using Trello with their personal Gmail to manage client projects or storing sensitive files in their personal Dropbox instead of your company's shared drive.

The danger here isn't that your team is trying to undermine you. It's that when things go wrong, *you don't know where to look*. If someone leaves or a system fails, and the tool they were using wasn't officially part of your workflow, you're completely in the dark. You can't secure what you don't know exists.

Even the most trustworthy employee can unintentionally create blind spots that expose you to risk. Without centralized access and a

CHAPTER 2. CENTRALIZATION (AND
CONSOLIDATION) ARE CRITICAL

standardized tech stack, there's no way to confirm what data you've lost — or even that you lost it at all.

Real-World Example: When Your Email List Walks Out the Door

A marketing agency had a junior employee running all their client newsletters through a personal Mailchimp account. When that employee left, they took the login with them — and locked the agency out of all client email lists. There was no admin recovery, no shared credentials, and no legal pathway to force access. Even though that employee left under amicable terms, they still didn't respond to requests from the agency for help getting back into the account. In the end, the agency had to rebuild everything from scratch and eat the loss.

Centralization isn't about controlling. It's about **protecting your business' data and continuity**. If you don't own your systems, you don't own your business.

Centralized Control vs. Shadow IT

Email ownership

- Shadow IT chaos: Personal Gmail or Outlook accounts
- Centralized control setup: Business-managed accounts (Google/M365)

Password control

- Shadow IT chaos: Stored in browsers, memory, or personal apps
- Centralized control setup: Password manager with admin access

Support access

♦ Shadow IT chaos: No admin access = no vendor support

♦ Centralized control setup: Admin credentials to open tickets and request recovery

File storage

♦ Shadow IT chaos: Dropbox, Box, USB drives — no central oversight

♦ Centralized control setup: Shared drives with audit logs and role-based access

Offboarding process

♦ Shadow IT chaos: Scattered logins, lost data, unknown access points

♦ Centralized control setup: Remove user access in minutes

Audit and compliance

♦ Shadow IT chaos: No logs, no visibility, no compliance readiness

♦ Centralized control setup: Visibility into tools, usage, and access levels

This information is often what convinces business owners to stop putting off the switch and start locking down their IT footprint.

Why GoDaddy (or Personal Gmails) for Your Business Email Is a Terrible Idea

At first glance, bundling email with your domain purchase seems convenient: one login, one vendor, one less thing to manage. But what you gain in simplicity up front, you pay tenfold later.

Here's what's really happening behind the curtain:

- ◆ **Limited admin console:** GoDaddy doesn't give you full access to the Microsoft 365 admin center. You're using a stripped-down interface with fewer tools for managing users, roles, security settings, and device policies. **Corollary:** These limitations also include more trouble including third-party backup solutions into your tech stack, leaving you more vulnerable to data loss.

- ◆ **Reduced support capabilities:** When you hit a technical snag, GoDaddy support might not even be able to escalate issues the same way Microsoft can. You're a customer of *GoDaddy*, not Microsoft.

- ◆ **Migration nightmares:** Moving off GoDaddy's platform is harder than it should be. Accounts are sometimes bundled in strange ways, and you'll often lose historic email logs, permissions settings, or aliases if the transition isn't handled carefully.

- ◆ **No real audit visibility:** You don't get true logging, mailbox access reports, or granular data control, which are crucial features if you're scaling or aiming for compliance.

- ◆ **Security tradeoffs:** GoDaddy-hosted Microsoft email accounts often miss out on premium security and compliance tools that come standard in a full Microsoft tenant.

And this is all assuming you decide to use a registrar to host your email. There are also the businesses who decide to pinch pennies and open free Gmail or Hotmail accounts to house critical business communications. Despite the already mentioned risks, nearly half of small businesses still used free personal email accounts or email bundled with their domain registrar as of 2015.[5] (In my experience, this may have dropped a little in the last 10 years. But not by much.) This erodes credibility and introduces serious security and deliverability challenges.

Real-World Example: When "Bonus" Email Hosting Costs You the Client

One of our clients needed to disable a terminated employee's email immediately. But because their Microsoft 365 account was hosted via GoDaddy, they didn't have the admin rights to do it. GoDaddy support quoted them a two- to three-business-day turnaround just to reassign admin roles. That delay led to a breach in client confidentiality and nearly lost them a major account.

Bottom line? Buy your domain from a registrar but host your email with a real email provider. Domain companies sell email hosting as a "bonus," but it's not designed for real business use.

Commit to One Storage System (Google Drive vs. SharePoint vs. Box) ... and NOT Dropbox

Using more than one storage platform might feel flexible at first. But, over time, it creates confusion, duplication, and risk. File sprawl isn't just annoying — it's *dangerous*.

A Cautionary Tale

A consulting firm had files scattered across multiple platforms: Dropbox for internal files, Box for one specific client, and Google Drive for everything else. No one could remember where anything lived. Some files had three versions and others were never backed up. Sharing with external clients turned into a scavenger hunt.

The real issue came during a client audit. A time-sensitive document had been updated in Dropbox, but only the outdated version in Google Drive was sent to the client. It nearly cost them the contract.

After the audit scare, they consolidated everything into Box, which was chosen for its compliance features and granular permission settings. Shared links were disabled unless approved, folders were standardized, and each user had role-based access. It wasn't just neater — it was safer.

Pick a Platform and Stick With It

♦ **Google Drive (via Google Workspace):** Great for real-time collaboration, easy search, and clean UI. Works especially well if you're already using Gmail and Google Calendar.

♦ **SharePoint (via Microsoft 365):** Ideal for structured internal documents, version control, and Teams integration. Best if your organization is already "Microsoft first."

♦ **Box:** Strongest choice for regulated industries (HIPAA, FINRA) or teams needing tight governance controls. Just don't use it as a bolt-on for one client. Commit or don't.

Dropbox, by contrast, lacks reliable backup integrations and the permission granularity needed for modern business use. It's time to move on. (More on this topic under "Why Dropbox Is Not a Backup Tool" in Chapter 3. "Back Up Before You Blackout.")

Here's a quick comparison to help you decide which one fits your business best:

File Storage Platform Comparison

Google Drive (Google Workspace)

♦ Advantages: Real-time collaboration, simplicity

♦ UI and usability: Intuitive, user-friendly

♦ Permission control: Role-based in Shared Drives

♦ Compliance features: HIPAA (with BAA), SOC 2, GDPR

♦ Backup integration: Spanning, Backupify

♦ Admin console: Full Google Workspace admin access

♦ Common pitfalls: Confusion between My Drive and Shared Drives

SharePoint (Microsoft 365)

♦ Advantages: Structured internal systems

♦ UI and usability: Steeper learning curve

♦ Permission control: Group/role-based via Sites

♦ Compliance features: HIPAA, FINRA, SOC 2, advanced DLP

♦ Backup integration: Spanning, Backupify

♦ Admin console: Spanning, Dropsuite, Veeam

♦ Common pitfalls: Permissions can get complex quickly, confusion between OneDrive and SharePoint

Box (Business/Enterprise)

♦ Advantages: Regulated industries, governance

♦ UI and usability: Moderate, more enterprise-focused

♦ Permission control: Highly granular with advanced controls

♦ Compliance features: HIPAA, FINRA, GDPR, strong audit tools

- Backup integration: CloudAlly, OwnBackup (limited tools), Box Governance add-on
- Admin console: Enterprise admin dashboard
- Common pitfalls: Pricey and overkill for very small teams

Use this information to match your storage choice with your current (and future) needs. Simpler is better — until it isn't. Choose the tool that will scale with your business, not just the one that feels familiar today.

Case Stories: When Too Many Tools Become the Problem

This chapter illustrates the hidden costs of an unstructured, overly flexible tech stack. The stories below highlight the pain of disorganization and the payoff of thoughtful centralization.

Coaching Agency: Tool Soup and Staff Burnout

Background: A coaching company with 14 part-time coaches had no centralized tech platform. The owner let each coach use whatever they were comfortable with: Some used Gmail; others Outlook. File sharing happened via a mix of Dropbox, Google Drive, and even WhatsApp attachments. Billing was handled through a separate tool. Passwords? Everyone kept their own.

The Problem: As the team grew, so did the chaos. Documents went missing. Client billing was delayed. One coach accidentally deleted an entire folder, and no one knew who had a backup. The final straw came when a client complained about receiving three different onboarding emails from three different platforms.

The Fix: The owner brought in an IT company to unify everything. They migrated to Google Workspace, set up Shared Drives, implemented LastPass for Business, and used Zapier to integrate appointment scheduling and CRM workflows.

The Outcome: Within a month, the coaches were operating from a single platform. Onboarding was standardized. Documents were always available. The owner even cut their tech tool spending by 38%.

Lesson Learned: Freedom without structure creates friction. The right constraints can unlock scale.

Architectural Firm: Order From Chaos

Background: A boutique architectural firm with a staff of six had grown quickly over two years. They used Microsoft 365 through GoDaddy, relied on personal Gmail accounts for calendar sharing, and shared project files in Dropbox using a single login across all staff.

The Problem: One designer accidentally deleted the firm's current project files during a Dropbox sync error. Because everyone used a single account, it was impossible to know who did what — or restore the right version. Calendar invites were often missed, and Outlook kept disconnecting from their project management tool.

The Fix: Their new IT provider migrated them to Google Workspace, set up Shared Drives with permission-based access, and standardized all users on Gmail and Google Calendar. They moved to Box for long-term client archiving and added Spanning for backups.

The Outcome: File errors dropped to zero. Onboarding new staff became plug-and-play. Meetings were no longer missed, and clients noticed the difference in professionalism.

Lesson Learned: When your tools talk to each other, your business starts to flow. When they don't, you're always working uphill.

The TL;DR

♦ Centralization is the first real step toward scalability.

♦ Choose one core platform (Google Workspace or Microsoft 365) and commit to it.

♦ Avoid tool sprawl. It wastes time, creates risk, and blocks growth.

♦ Always use admin-controlled business accounts. Never run your company off personal emails.

♦ Keep your cloud storage and email platform consistent whenever possible. Don't mix and match (And, for goodness sake, don't use Dropbox.)

♦ Registrars are for domains, not email or website hosting.

See a list of free resources under Appendix C. "Resources."

Now that you've laid the groundwork for centralizing your tools and systems, it's time to confront one of the biggest blind spots in small business IT: assuming cloud storage is the same as backup. (Spoiler alert: It's not.)

Next up, we'll show you how to build real resilience with a layered backup strategy.

CHAPTER 3

Back Up Before You Blackout

Cloud Storage Is Not a Backup

Let's get one thing straight: Cloud storage is not a backup. If that's the first time you've heard that, don't worry — you're in good company.

Most small business owners assume that because their files show up in Dropbox, OneDrive, or Google Drive, they're "backed up." But, in reality, those platforms are syncing files, not backing them up. If something gets deleted, overwritten, or encrypted by ransomware, those changes are all faithfully replicated to the cloud, meaning that you're not looking at a safety net — you're looking at a black hole.

Here's the really crappy part: All of the vendors (including the ones we recommend, like Dropbox, Google, and Microsoft) confuse the issue with terrible terminology and half-truths ("Back up your files with Dropbox!"), so it's no wonder that you come away thinking you're protected when you're really not.

The only situation where this acts like a backup is when your computer crashes. When you get a new computer and log in, you see all your files still there. *That's it.*

The "Oh, !@#$" Moment Every Business Eventually Has

At some point, everyone hits that "Oops" moment:

- ◆ A contractor deletes the wrong folder.
- ◆ A staffer overwrites a critical doc with an old version.
- ◆ A phishing email slips through, and ransomware locks you out of everything.

When that happens, the clock starts ticking. Every hour lost is money, momentum, and reputation out the window. Without a proper backup solution, you're gambling every day.

And if you're gambling that you'll catch the mistake in time? Guess again. Most data loss happens when something gets deleted and it isn't needed again for months, after which the cloud storage "trash bin" doesn't have those files anymore. Statistically, if you delete files by accident, you won't notice until it's too late.

It's alarming how few small businesses plan for worst-case scenarios. Roughly 75% don't have any kind of DRP in place.[6] That's not just risky. It's a ticking time bomb.

What Real Backup Looks Like

A proper backup strategy includes these key traits:

- ◆ **Separate infrastructure:** Your backup should live outside the system it's protecting. If your data is in Google Workspace, the backup should be on a different system entirely.

- **Version history:** Your strategy should include the ability to roll back not just to yesterday's version but to any point in time (say, before malware got in).

- **Admin-controlled restores:** You — not just your employees and not just your vendor — should be able to trigger a recovery quickly, cleanly, and completely.

Why We Love (and Use) Spanning

For businesses using Google Workspace or Microsoft 365, Spanning by Kaseya is one of the best backup tools around. It's simple, reliable, and made specifically for these platforms. It backs up:

- Email
- Contacts
- Calendars
- Drive or OneDrive files
- SharePoint sites and Teams

And it does it automatically, with flexible restore options that don't require calling tech support every time you need to fix something.

This is the type of "set it and sleep better" tool you want in your corner.

Spanning is a tool we use for our clients, but there are others you can also seek out. Backupify by Datto is another similar tool, and FINRA-regulated companies often get a lot of value out of Smarsh's offerings as well.

Why Dropbox Is Not a Backup Tool

Let's say it loud for the folks in the back: **Dropbox is not a backup.** It syncs files between your devices. That means:

- If you delete a file on your laptop, it disappears from Dropbox too.

- If you overwrite a file, the old version is gone forever unless you have a paid plan *and catch it in time.*

- If ransomware hits, Dropbox can — and will — sync the encrypted files across all devices before you can blink.

This isn't to say that Dropbox is evil. It just wasn't built for secure business continuity. And relying on it for backup is like using duct tape for plumbing: It might work until it really, *really* doesn't.

Nearly 40% of small businesses reported losing crucial data as a result of a cyberattack.[7] That's not just files. It's customer records, financials, even operations coming to a standstill.

Layer Your Backup Strategy

A smart backup plan uses layers. Think of it like a seatbelt and an airbag:

- Use platform-native versioning (like Google's file history or SharePoint's revision tracking) for quick saves.

- Add a third-party backup tool like Spanning for full recovery and compliance.

- If you have sensitive data, consider encrypting and archiving long-term backups offsite or in cold storage.

Redundancy isn't waste; it's resilience. Most businesses (93%) that suffer extended data loss — 10 days or more — go bankrupt within a year.[8] Without a reliable backup strategy, you're one crash or breach away from total shutdown.

The Three Tiers of Backup

Most small businesses think having *any* backup is enough. But that's like thinking a spare tire means you don't need insurance or roadside assistance. Real resilience comes from layered recovery options.

Tier 1: Local Backup (external hard drives, local NAS)

- ☑ Fast recovery
- ✗ Risk: fire, theft, ransomware, hardware failure

Tier 2: Cloud Backup (Backblaze, CrashPlan)

- ☑ Offsite, encrypted, automatic
- ✗ Requires internet access, sometimes slower recovery
- ✗ Doesn't back up cloud storage files found in Dropbox, OneDrive, and more to be expanded over time

Tier 3: SaaS-Level Backup + Versioning (Spanning, Datto)

- ☑ Critical for Google Workspace/M365
- ☑ Protects email, calendars, Google Drive, OneDrive, and more to be expanded over time
- ☑ Supports version rollback and retention policies

Regardless of your size, **never rely on only one layer**. Backup isn't the plan — it's the parachute.

The 3-2-1 Backup Rule

Here's a great rule to keep in mind:

- ♦ **3** copies of your data
- ♦ **2** different types of storage (cloud + external drive)
- ♦ **1** or more copies stored offsite or offline

This rule applies to critical data (client records, financial info, signed contracts), not your lunch-order history.

Case Stories: What Happens When You Don't Have a Plan

This section shows a couple of stark outcomes: one business that lost everything due to a single point of failure, and another business that suffered an attack but had the right safety net in place.

The Surgical Practice That Didn't Come Back

Background: A well-established surgical practice, operating for over 15 years, was managing all of its IT internally. They didn't have an IT provider and were relying on basic systems they had set up themselves. The owner believed he was protected because he had a backup system in place.

The Problem: One day, the practice was hit by a ransomware attack. All data on the main workstation — containing PII and PHI — was encrypted. The owner thought he was safe thanks to backups, but those backups were stored on a locally attached hard drive. It was connected to the infected machine, which meant the ransomware encrypted that too. This violated HIPAA standards and rendered both the primary and backup data completely unusable. There were no cloud backups. No recovery point. No options.

The Fix: There wasn't one. I was called in, but there was nothing I could do. The only theoretical option was to pay the ransom and hope the attackers would restore access — something that only happens about 25% of the time.

The Outcome: I never spoke to the owner again. But I remember that call. He wasn't the emotional type. But, as he realized what had happened, he choked up and said, "My entire livelihood is here."

Knowing the stats (two-thirds of small businesses fail after a breach) and knowing his data was gone, it was likely the end of his practice.

Lesson Learned: A backup is not a backup if it's exposed to the same risk as the original. One workstation is not a server. One copy is not a plan. The moment you realized you needed layers was the moment you should have had them in place. And, by then, it's too late.

Engineering Consultancy: Disaster Dodged

Background: A 12-person structural engineering consultancy worked with an IT provider to implement Spanning for Google Workspace, off-site backups for their CAD systems, and a full incident-response plan.

The Problem: A ransomware variant hit one of their admin accounts. The attack was contained before spreading, but several folders were still encrypted.

The Fix: Within hours, they restored clean versions of the affected files from their backups. Their IT provider handled communications, containment, and documentation. No data was lost, and no ransom was paid.

The Outcome: Clients were notified transparently, but none left. The firm completed their projects on time, filed the incident with their cyber insurance provider, and used the situation as a springboard to train staff further.

Lesson Learned: You don't rise to the occasion — you fall to your level of preparation. Their systems were ready, so their business stayed ready.

The TL;DR

♦ Sync ≠ backup. They serve different purposes.

- ◆ Every business hits a "we lost it" moment. Be ready for yours.

- ◆ Backups should live outside your primary system and be controlled by you.

- ◆ Spanning is a fantastic backup tool for Google Workspace and Microsoft 365.

- ◆ Dropbox is not a secure backup solution. Using it that way is asking for trouble.

- ◆ Layer your backups like you'd layer your defenses. Sometimes, you don't get a second chance.

You've got your data backed up and your systems starting to look solid. But what happens if things still go sideways? Here's the truth: No setup is bulletproof. That's where cyber liability insurance comes in.

In the next chapter, we'll explore how to protect not just your files but your finances and reputation too.

CHAPTER 4

Cyber Liability Insurance: Your Financial Firewall

What Happens If You Get Hit?

Let's say you've done everything right: You've got backups, secure tools, and a killer IT setup. Great! Now ask yourself: *"What happens if I still get hit?"*

Here's the dirty secret no one likes to talk about: **You can do everything right and still get hacked.** Maybe it's a zero-day exploit. Maybe an employee falls for a perfectly crafted phishing email. Maybe it's just dumb luck. The point is: *Insurance exists for a reason.*

Why General Liability Isn't Enough

Most small businesses assume their general business liability insurance covers everything, including cyber events. *It doesn't.*

General liability covers physical damage, bodily injury, and maybe some basic business interruption. It does *not* cover:

- Costs to recover encrypted or stolen data
- Legal fees related to breach investigations
- Fines for violating privacy laws or compliance standards (HIPAA, FINRA)
- Customer notification and credit monitoring
- Public relations or reputation management after a breach

If you think cybercriminals only target big names, think again: Almost half (43%) of all cyberattacks are aimed at small businesses like yours.[9] That's why even your tech-stack design needs to factor in security from day one. You need **cyber liability insurance** to handle those things. *Full stop.*

What Cyber Insurance Actually Covers

Cyber liability insurance isn't about covering your computer. It's about covering your *business*. At its core, a solid policy helps recover from financial and reputational fallout after a digital disaster. But, like any insurance, it's only useful if you understand what it actually does (and doesn't) cover.

Here are some of the most common things cyber liability insurance *does* cover:

- **Data breach costs:** Notifying affected clients, offering credit monitoring, and hiring breach counsel
- **Ransomware response:** Paying a ransom (if permitted by law), data recovery, and negotiations
- **Business interruption:** Lost income due to downtime caused by an attack
- **Incident response services:** IT forensics, legal help, PR firms, and more to be expanded over time

♦ **Regulatory fines and legal defense:** If you're sued or fined for data mishandling or noncompliance

But here's the thing: **Coverage depends on your policy.** Some policies exclude phishing attacks unless MFA is in place. Some require proof of proper backup systems. Others might not cover insider threats or third-party vendor breaches unless specific riders are added.

And many people wrongly assume general business liability insurance covers these kinds of events. It used to, but it doesn't anymore, so it's important to review your current insurance policies on a regular basis for this kind of reason. Cyber incidents are usually explicitly excluded in those policies.

Cyber insurance is there to help when your systems get breached, your data gets locked, or your clients are notified that their information was exposed. It's not magic, and it doesn't prevent the incident from happening. But it can absolutely keep you from going under after it does.

What Cyber Insurance Covers vs. What It Doesn't (Usually)

Covered (Usually)

♦ Data breach notification and response

♦ Ransomware recovery costs

♦ Downtime and business interruption

♦ Regulatory fines and legal fees

♦ Forensic and legal investigations

Not Covered (Usually)

♦ Preexisting security issues

- Failure to *maintain* required security controls
- Acts of war or state-sponsored cyber attacks
- Employee negligence (unless explicitly covered)
- Non-IT losses (lost reputation alone)

Policies are getting more nuanced. Good ones are flexible, but they still come with exclusions, conditions, and fine print. Make sure your broker explains what's not covered just as clearly as what *is*.

Why It Matters What Cyber Liability Insurance Actually Covers

A law firm I worked with had their files locked up by ransomware one Monday morning. They had good backups and a reliable IT provider, so the damage was *mostly* contained. But the firm still had to disclose the breach due to the type of client data involved.

Here's where the insurance came in:

- It paid for legal counsel to help navigate state notification laws.
- It covered the PR firm that helped them draft and distribute client notifications.
- It reimbursed them for downtime and billable hours lost during the recovery.
- It paid for a forensic team to make sure the attack was fully contained.

They didn't lose a single client.

Why? Because their response was fast, transparent, and well-resourced — **thanks to the policy they'd put in place six months earlier**.

Now compare that to another business I spoke with: same situation but no insurance. They didn't know how to respond. They fumbled communications. And they absorbed the full cost out of pocket. The owner told me, "If we'd had coverage, I wouldn't have lost my biggest account and wouldn't have had to let go of two people."

The price of a misstep can be enormous. The average cyberattack on a small business costs between $120,000 and $150,000.[10] That's a massive bill for cutting corners on IT planning.

Cyber insurance isn't a luxury. It's a safety net you *hope* you'll never need — but you'll be glad it's there when you do.

How to Shop for a Policy without Getting Screwed

Let's get real. Most small business owners don't know how to vet cyber insurance brokers. And most brokers? They don't know squat about IT. They're generalists pushing policies written for big companies or bundling cyber coverage into a larger umbrella policy with very little detail.

Here's how to avoid getting burned.

Vet Your Broker Like You Vet a Lawyer

◆ Do they specialize in cyber liability?

◆ Can they explain what's covered and what isn't without hiding behind jargon?

◆ Will they walk you through the *application process*, including technical requirements?

◆ Do they have experience working with small, professional services firms?

If they only sell through big consumer names like State Farm or Allstate, keep moving. Those carriers are great for general business insurance but not cyber liability.

Look for a broker or provider that:

♦ Works with multiple carriers and can compare options

♦ Understands the difference between "claims made" vs. "occurrence" policies

♦ Will explain what triggers a payout (and what disqualifies you)

Broker Red Flags

♦ They assure you, "Don't worry, you're covered!" with no detailed explanation.

♦ They can't show you a sample policy or explain the exclusions.

♦ They try to *bundle* your cyber liability into a larger general policy without breaking out the terms.

♦ They don't ask about MFA, backups, or IT policies, which all affect your eligibility.

PRO TIP

Even if they're not the final provider for your business, Datastream Insurance is a great place to get a baseline or second opinion. They specialize in small businesses and know what underwriters are really looking for.

The bottom line? Don't shop for cyber insurance like it's just another checkbox. Shop for it like your business depends on it because, one day, it just might. ●

Why It (and IT) Should Be in Your Budget EVERY Year

Think of cyber liability insurance and IT managed services as a one-two punch. Each is strong on its own. But, together, they're the combination that knocks out serious risk.

Your IT vendor or MSP is the one installing security software, patching vulnerabilities, running backups, and training your staff. That's proactive. But, no matter how good your IT is, it can't guarantee 100% protection. That's where cyber insurance comes in. It's your financial safety net when things go sideways.

And here's the kicker: They actually complement each other beautifully:

- Having solid IT practices (MFA, backups, documented policies) can **lower your insurance premiums**.

- Good cyber insurance policies often **require** you to have those IT practices in place to qualify or receive full payout.

- If you work with a broker who understands security, they can help shape your IT strategy based on what underwriters want to see.

It's a virtuous cycle: better IT > better insurance > better resilience > lower long-term cost.

This shouldn't be a "this or that" decision. It should always be **both**.

RULE OF THUMB

If you're budgeting for IT at all (and you should be), cyber insurance should be right alongside it. Think of it as a fixed annual line item, just like payroll or office rent. •

For most professional services firms:

♦ Cyber insurance can cost as little as **$1,000 to $2,500/year**, depending on size, industry, and IT posture.

♦ Compare that to the **$100,000+** it could cost if you're breached without coverage.

Plan for it. Bake it in. Sleep easier knowing it's there when you need it.

What Your Cyber Policy *Should* Include

Not all cyber policies are created equal, and some are barely worth the paper they're written on.

Here's a checklist of key components to look for in a **solid cyber liability policy**:

♦ **First-party coverage:** Covers your own losses and expenses (breach response, ransomware, business interruption, forensic investigations)

♦ **Third-party liability:** Covers claims made against your business from clients, vendors, or regulators

♦ **Data breach response costs:** Covers legal notifications, credit monitoring, PR crisis management, and compliance support

♦ **Cyber extortion/ransomware coverage:** Covers ransom payments (where legal), data recovery, and negotiation services

♦ **Business interruption coverage:** Pays out for lost income when your systems are unusable due to an attack

♦ **Contingent business interruption:** Covers you when a vendor's system outage or breach impacts your operations

- **Social engineering fraud coverage:** Specifically covers losses due to scams like wire fraud and phishing — even if you "approved" the transaction

- **Regulatory fines and legal costs:** Includes legal defense and fines from government agencies if your breach violates HIPAA, GDPR, or state laws

- **Breach coach or incident response team access:** Provides expert guidance when you're in crisis mode. These folks help you navigate legal, technical, and PR landmines

My Broker Said I'm Covered. Am I?

This one's tricky because many brokers *genuinely believe* they're selling you solid cyber coverage. But, unless they specialize in this space, what they're offering might fall painfully short when things go wrong. Only 14% of small businesses are actually prepared to handle a cyber-attack.[11] So, even if you *think* you've got the basics in place, it's worth revisiting your policies and your tech stack with this in mind.

Here are a few common traps:

- **Bundled cyber coverage in general policies:** Many small business policies now include a token amount of cyber liability coverage (usually $25K to $100K). That sounds fine until you realize a real incident could cost 10 times that.

- **"Silent Cyber" clauses:** Some general liability or E&O policies used to quietly cover cyber incidents. Not anymore. Many now *explicitly exclude* anything that smells like a breach or digital attack.

- **Lack of technical questions:** If your broker didn't ask you anything about backups, MFA, IT policies, or vendor access, you can bet the underwriter didn't price your policy accurately. That's a problem for you at *claim time*.

♦ **No clarity on exclusions:** If the policy doesn't spell out "social engineering fraud" or "ransomware coverage" in black and white, assume it's not included.

Here's a quick test: Ask your broker, "What scenarios would *not* be covered under this policy?" If they can't answer that quickly and clearly, it's a red flag.

You don't need to become an insurance expert. But you *do* need to ask pointed questions and work with someone who actually understands what today's cyber threats look like.

How to Get Denied (and Not Even Know It)

Nothing stings like assuming you're covered only to have your claim denied when you need it most. Cyber insurance has some very specific requirements, and failing to meet them can void your policy faster than you think.

Here are some of the most common reasons businesses get denied:

♦ **No MFA:** MFA is the bare minimum standard today. If it's not enabled on email, backups, or remote access, your claim could be denied outright.

♦ **Lack of a backup system:** If you can't demonstrate a secure, verifiable backup plan (with retention history), insurers may refuse to pay for recovery costs.

♦ **Failure to patch known vulnerabilities:** If the breach came through outdated software or unpatched systems, and you had reasonable ability to fix it beforehand, that's on you.

- **No incident-response plan:** Some policies require you to act quickly and follow a defined incident process. If you fumble that response or delay key steps, you could lose eligibility.

- **Inaccurate or incomplete application information:** If you claimed you use a password manager but you don't, or said you conduct security training but haven't, your claim could be tossed out under the heading of "misrepresentation."

Think of your cyber policy like a conditional agreement. You're agreeing to uphold a basic standard of IT hygiene. If you don't? The insurer doesn't have to uphold their end either.

Case Stories: Cyber Liability Insurance in the Real World

These stories show both ends of the cyber insurance spectrum: one company that had all the boxes checked but missed a critical control, and one that had their policy *and* security in sync.

Financial Advisory Firm: All But One

Background: A seven-person financial advisory group had cyber liability insurance, an internal IT lead, and policies that *mostly* aligned with their insurer's requirements.

The Problem: One employee had managed to disable MFA on their account for convenience. That one account became the entry point for a phishing attack that led to wire fraud. Because MFA enforcement was listed as a requirement in their policy — and wasn't universally applied — their insurer denied the claim.

The Fix: The business had to eat the cost. They reengaged their IT provider to harden all accounts and underwent an extensive review of their security posture.

The Outcome: Trust was shaken, and the incident nearly cost them two major clients. Their IT oversight had been just good enough to seem safe but not good enough to hold up when it mattered.

Lesson Learned: Cyber insurance is not a substitute for security. It's a partner to it. One gap can nullify the safety net.

Engineering Firm: Strategy That Paid Off

Background: A 16-person structural engineering company had worked with their IT provider and insurance broker to align security policies with insurance expectations.

The Problem: After a compromised vendor system forwarded malware to their inboxes, a team member clicked a spoofed invoice link. The infection was caught by IRONSCALES, but a few internal systems were briefly exposed.

The Fix: Their backups were verified. Legal counsel and PR assistance were engaged under their cyber policy's incident-response clause. The insurer covered the investigation and cleanup — and even paid for client notifications.

The Outcome: There was no long-term damage. Clients praised the firm's fast, professional handling of the situation.

Lesson Learned: The best cyber policies are paired with well-run IT systems. Insurance pays off *when you're ready to meet it halfway*.

The TL;DR

- Cyber insurance doesn't protect your systems. It protects your business *after* a breach.

♦ A good policy should cover breach response, ransomware, legal defense, business interruption, and more to be expanded over time.

♦ Just having a policy isn't enough. You need the right *security controls* in place (like MFA and backups) or your claim can be denied.

♦ Brokers who aren't cyber specialists may sell you inadequate or bundled policies. Ask tough questions.

♦ Cyber insurance and managed IT services are a one-two punch. IT prevents the damage. Insurance helps recover from it.

♦ Common ways to get denied include no MFA, outdated software, missing backups, or incorrect info on your application.

♦ Even one staff member turning off MFA can invalidate the whole policy. And yes, that has happened.

♦ You don't need to become an insurance expert. But you *do* need to understand what you're buying and what responsibilities come with it.

♦ Don't wait until something breaks to find out if you're covered. Know now, adjust now, and sleep better because of it.

You're thinking like a leader, budgeting smartly, and preparing for the unexpected. Now let's get specific about how to secure your systems.

In the next chapter, guest author Niko Nikolaidis introduces the NIST cybersecurity framework and explains why even the smallest businesses should care.

PART II

Security, Control, and Digital Hygiene

NIST Standards: What, Why, and How to Implement Them

The Mentality of NIST

Niko here! This chapter is all me.

Growing up in a family that owned restaurants, I was exposed to the inner workings of running a successful business. At the end of each day, I remember my father keeping his records in ledger books and storing receipts in marked envelopes, which would then be locked in a safe. A simple method to track all the sales, vendor information, and other important data for day-to-day necessities. This was back in the '80s and '90s. Not a single computer on the premises. The registers were little more than preprogrammed calculators that printed receipts. He easily kept track of everything in his books and memory. An alarm with a locked gate, paper and pen, and said registers were all the technology he needed to keep things going. Those were simpler days ...

Now, in today's world with ever-evolving technologies being incorporated into just about every aspect of our lives, it is easy to get lost and lose track of every morsel of these technologies. Remembering passwords for email accounts and bank accounts, different logins for various accounts as well as for each of our multiple devices — all are just the very tip of the iceberg. Let alone what to do if we forget them or, dare I say, get hacked or compromised.

Building a mentality to keep track of everything and prevent exposure, monitoring, and reacting when things go wrong are all necessary skills to keep your digital architecture from collapsing and maintain a successful business. Physical keys and a safe with records simply do not cut it in our modern era. That is why I feel it is important to share with you a framework that provides the building blocks to an organized and secure infrastructure.

What Is NIST?

The NIST is a US government agency under the Department of Commerce. While best known for developing cybersecurity and technical standards for federal agencies and contractors, its frameworks are increasingly used by private businesses to manage risk and build resilient digital environments.

NIST guidelines are **free, publicly available**, and designed to be **flexible** for businesses of all sizes. (See "Resources" at the end of this chapter for links!)

Why NIST Matters for Small Businesses

Small businesses are frequently targeted by cybercriminals because:

- They often lack strong security practices.
- They store sensitive data (customer info, credit cards, healthcare records).

CHAPTER 5. NIST STANDARDS: WHAT, WHY, AND HOW TO IMPLEMENT THEM

- They serve as entry points to larger supply chains.

Adopting a framework like NIST provides:

- A **structured approach** to cybersecurity.
- Increased **trust** with customers and partners.
- Support for **compliance** with industry and government regulations.

The NIST Cybersecurity Framework

The NIST CSF is a beginner-friendly model made up the following functional pillars:

- "Identify" Pillar: Understand your business assets and risks.
- "Protect" Pillar: Put controls in place to defend against threats.
- "Detect" Pillar: Monitor for and discover incidents quickly.
- "Respond" Pillar: Take action when something goes wrong.
- "Recover" Pillar: Restore services and reduce long-term damage.

Step-by-Step Application

Here's how your business can align with the CSF:

"Identify" Pillar

- **Inventory all** computers, devices, software, and cloud platforms.
- Map where your sensitive data is stored and who can access it.
- Conduct a basic risk assessment. What data would be most damaging to lose?

You can see examples of this pillar in the following chapters:

- Chapter 2. "Centralization (and Consolidation) Are Critical"
- Chapter 8. "Build Workflows That Scale with You"
- Chapter 11. "Your Machines Age: Know How to Budget and When to Upgrade"
- Chapter 13. "The IT Growth Plan: From 1 to 20 and Beyond"
- Chapter 14. "Remote Work Done Right: IT for Distributed Teams"
- Chapter 15. "Where HR Meets IT: Security, Monitoring, and Onboarding"

"Protect" Pillar

- Use antivirus software and firewalls.
- Require strong passwords and MFA.
- Apply software updates regularly.
- **Train staff** in basic cybersecurity hygiene.

You can see examples of this pillar in the following chapters:

- Chapter 4. "Cyber Liability Insurance: Your Financial Firewall"
- Chapter 6. "Security That Scales"
- Chapter 7. "User Access and Risk Management"
- Chapter 9. "SaaS That Works for the 1-20 Crowd"
- Chapter 11. "Your Machines Age: Know How to Budget and When to Upgrade"
- Chapter 12. "When (and How) to Outsource IT the Smart Way"
- Chapter 13. "The IT Growth Plan: From 1 to 20 and Beyond"
- Chapter 14. "Remote Work Done Right: IT for Distributed Teams"

CHAPTER 5. NIST STANDARDS: WHAT, WHY, AND HOW TO IMPLEMENT THEM

♦ Chapter 15. "Where HR Meets IT: Security, Monitoring, and Onboarding"

"Detect" Pillar

♦ Enable alerts for suspicious login attempts or software changes.

♦ Monitor network activity. Many routers and security tools offer this by default.

♦ Consider lightweight **log management tools** or security platforms.

You can see examples of this pillar in the following chapters:

♦ Chapter 15. "Where HR Meets IT: Security, Monitoring, and Onboarding"

♦ Chapter 16. "Regulated But Resilient: IT for Compliance-Heavy Industries"

"Respond" Pillar

♦ Draft a **simple incident response plan** (who to contact and steps to take).

♦ Designate an internal or external **IT lead** for crisis events.

♦ Document all responses for future improvement and liability protection.

You can see examples of this pillar in the following chapters:

♦ Chapter 7. "User Access and Risk Management"

♦ Chapter 10. "Plan for the Worst (So You Can Stay at Your Best)"

♦ Chapter 17. "Bonus Case Studies: What It Looks Like in the Wild"

"Recover" Pillar

- Perform **daily backups** of business-critical data.
- Test restoration regularly.
- Use findings from incidents to strengthen your systems.

You can see examples of this pillar in the following chapters:

- Chapter 3. "Back Up Before You Blackout"
- Chapter 10. "Plan for the Worst (So You Can Stay at Your Best)"
- Chapter 17. "Bonus Case Studies: What It Looks Like in the Wild"

What About NIST SP 800-171?

If your business deals with the federal government or handles CUI, you may need to follow NIST Special Publication 800-171. It outlines 14 families of requirements such as:

- Access Control
- Media Protection
- System Integrity
- Personnel Security
- Audit and Accountability

While this standard is more technical, small businesses can use it as a **blueprint** for building advanced security policies over time.

A Basic NIST-Based Small Business Security List

Use this list to apply NIST CSF basics in your IT setup:

- Inventory all devices, data, accounts, and software.
- Use strong passwords and MFA.

- ◆ Train employees on phishing and scams.
- ◆ Enable antivirus software, firewalls, and encryption.
- ◆ Back up critical data regularly.
- ◆ Create a simple incident-response plan.
- ◆ Review access permissions periodically.

Final Thoughts: Start Small, Scale Securely

Implementing NIST standards doesn't require a huge budget or a dedicated IT department. Start with the basics: Identify what needs protection, build simple safeguards, and grow from there.

By aligning with NIST, you:

- ◆ Build trust with clients and partners.
- ◆ Strengthen your ability to survive cyberattacks.
- ◆ Prepare your business for future growth and compliance needs.

Security is not a destination — it's a habit. Use NIST as your guide, and your small business can punch above its weight in cyber resilience.

You don't need a government contract to use NIST. Just a desire to run a safer business. Now that you've seen the framework, we'll zoom in on security tactics that actually work for small teams.

Up next: MFA, endpoint protection, phishing defense, and the habits that protect your business every day.

CHAPTER 6

Security That Scales

Security Mindset

Here's the truth about cybersecurity: **You don't need military-grade security, but you do need maturity.** Most small businesses aren't targeted by name, but they're vulnerable by design. And when your tools, people, and habits aren't secured properly, you're basically leaving the keys in the ignition.

The goal of this chapter is to help you implement **just enough security to grow confidently** without locking down your business like Fort Knox or overwhelming your team.

Start with MFA

Let's be clear: MFA isn't optional anymore. If you only do one thing after reading this chapter, *do this*. And, statistically, you aren't yet. Even though MFA is one of the most effective ways to block unauthorized access, adoption remains shockingly low — just 27% of businesses with 25 or fewer employees use it.[12] That means three out of four small businesses are leaving the front door wide open.

Yes, I've read the headlines too: Some attackers are finding ways to bypass it, and passkeys are on the horizon. But **right now**, MFA is still one of the single most important things you can do to protect your accounts.

Here's what MFA does: Even if someone steals your password, they can't log in unless they also have access to your phone, token, or biometric authentication. That one extra step stops most low-level attackers dead in their tracks.

Real-World Example: MFA Saved the Deal

A client received an email that looked exactly like a Google Workspace login screen. What was the only thing that saved them from handing over full access to their entire system? Their IT provider had enforced MFA. The attacker got the password but couldn't pass the second prompt. *End of story.*

That's what you want: a defense that stops the bad guys, even when you or your staff make a mistake.

With and Without MFA

Password stolen via phishing

- Without MFA: Full account compromise
- With MFA: Login attempt blocked

Employee uses same password everywhere

- Without MFA: All accounts potentially breached
- With MFA: Limited risk, MFA blocks unauthorized use

Admin account targeted in brute-force attacks

- Without MFA: Potential total access
- With MFA: Locked down unless 2nd factor bypassed

Phishing link clicked

- Without MFA: Credentials leaked, no barrier
- With MFA: Credentials leaked but attacker blocked

Enable MFA for any system that supports it, but *specifically do so for:*

- Google Workspace or Microsoft 365
- Password managers like LastPass
- File-storage platforms if located outside of Google Workspace or Microsoft 365 (see Chapter 2. "Centralization (and Consolidation) Are Critical" for warnings about doing this)
- Financial and banking tools
- CRMs and client portals

MFA isn't perfect, but it raises the bar *a lot*. And, if your insurance or IT policy requires it (which it probably does), it's nonnegotiable.

What "Remember This Device" Does

When you check the "Remember this device" box, the site typically sets a **persistent cookie** in your browser. This means that, for the duration specified (like 30 days), you won't be prompted for MFA on that device/browser combo again.

This is convenient, but it introduces potential **security risks** if not managed carefully.

When It's OK to Enable MFA

♦ **Trusted, company-managed devices:** If you're using MDM/RMM tools and endpoint protection

♦ **Low-risk apps:** Where compromise wouldn't lead to serious damage (an internal wiki)

♦ **Frequent logins:** Where MFA fatigue would be high otherwise (email clients like Outlook program) or CRMs used dozens of times a day

When You Shouldn't Use MFA

♦ **Shared or personal devices:** Never remember MFA on untrusted or unmanaged hardware.

♦ **High-risk systems:** Always require fresh MFA for admin consoles, cloud storage, financial platforms.

♦ **Browsers that don't autoclear cookies:** Anyone could bypass MFA just by opening your browser.

How to "Enforce It" Safely

♦ **Policy exceptions:** Use conditional access rules to "only allow device remembering" from company-issued machines or preregistered IP addresses.

♦ **Limit duration:** Some tools (Azure AD, Duo) let you set the remember period globally. Most cloud tools are standardized to 30 days, and you should generally avoid checking that "Remember" box since you can't adjust that timer.

♦ **Log it:** Know — and **document** — which devices are remembered and for how long.

How to "Audit It" Regularly

- **Review remembered devices:** Some platforms let you revoke them. Do this monthly or during offboarding.

- **Simulate compromise:** Try logging in from a new browser and device to make sure MFA is enforced.

- **Check for expired tokens:** Ensure old browser cookies/token sessions are invalidated after account changes or password resets.

Your Antivirus Software Is Not Enough Anymore

Gone are the days when a basic antivirus program could keep you safe. Modern threats evolve faster than traditional antivirus tools can keep up. If you're still using the same software from 2014, you're running with a blindfold on.

Worse? Many Mac users still don't run any antivirus software at all.

That's a huge risk. Modern malware is written for both Windows *and* macOS. And while Macs might be less targeted than Windows machines, they're not immune — especially in mixed environments or when users run browser-based apps that don't care what system you're using.

What you need now is EDR. Think of it as antivirus software with a brain:

- It doesn't just block known threats — it watches for suspicious behavior.

- It gives IT teams real-time alerts.

- It helps contain infections before they spread.

Tools like SentinelOne, Sophos Intercept X, or Microsoft Defender for Business bring this kind of intelligence to your endpoints (your staff's devices).

What Antivirus Software/EDR Should Do

- ◆ Detect and block malware and ransomware.
- ◆ Alert strange behavior (like scripts running where they shouldn't).
- ◆ Auto-isolate infected machines.
- ◆ Provide logging and reporting for audit or insurance purposes.

What Antivirus Software/EDR Won't Do

- ◆ Stop a phishing attack if someone hands over credentials.
- ◆ Patch outdated software.
- ◆ Manage backups.
- ◆ Enforce MFA.

It's one layer in your defense strategy, not the whole strategy. But skipping it, especially on Macs, is like leaving the barn door wide open and hoping the wolves don't notice.

Email Is Still the #1 Attack Vector

No matter how shiny your other defenses are, email remains the front door attackers keep knocking on — and often walk right through.

Why? Because email is where people make decisions. It's where they get tricked, rushed, and manipulated into clicking, downloading, or replying when they shouldn't.

Why Email Is So Dangerous

- ◆ It's used by everyone, every day.
- ◆ Most phishing emails are visually convincing.
- ◆ Hackers prey on urgency ("Your invoice is late," "Please review this document," or "Your account will be closed").
- ◆ People trust what they *think* they recognize.

Even with great spam filtering, **some attacks will always get through**. And, when they do, your team is the last line of defense.

The Skeleton Key to Everything

Your email account is the master key to your digital life. It's where you go to reset passwords. If someone gets access to your inbox, they can reset nearly any other account you own. Think about that.

If your staff shares passwords across services and their email gets popped? That attacker now has a map, a key, and an open invitation.

Modern Protection Requires Modern Tools

Tools like **IRONSCALES** go far beyond traditional spam filters. They learn what phishing looks like in your environment and — even better — they protect the whole team:

- ◆ When one person reports a phishing email, it can automatically quarantine the same email in everyone else's inbox.
- ◆ It builds what we call "herd immunity" for your business.

Combine this with **ongoing staff training** (yes, you have to do it) and strong password hygiene, and you've got a real shot at stopping email-based attacks before they sink the ship.

Passwords Are a Team Sport

Weak passwords don't just hurt individuals — they put the entire company at risk. If one person gets breached and their password also unlocks shared systems or tools? That breach just became everyone's problem.

Strong passwords aren't enough if they're stored on sticky notes or recycled across accounts. Yet only 46% of SMBs have a password management solution in place.[13] If your team doesn't have one, you're overdue.

The fix isn't more complexity. It's **centralization and visibility**.

Here's What Centralization and Visibility Look Like

- ◆ Use a team-grade password manager (LastPass Business, 1Password, Dashlane for Business)
- ◆ Store *all* credentials there (no spreadsheets, notepad files, or browser-saved passwords).
- ◆ Set up **shared vaults** or folders by department (sales, finance, and admin).
- ◆ Control access by role and remove access automatically during offboarding.

Turnover Made Simple

Without a password manager, offboarding is chaos. You have to manually reset every account you think the former employee had access to. If they stored passwords in their head — or worse, in a personal browser — you're guessing.

With a password manager:

- Disable their access to the vault.
- Reset only *one* master login (like email)
- Everything else is locked down immediately.

Unique Passwords Are Mandatory — But Easier Than You Think

If your staff still thinks they need to remember passwords, they'll reuse them — or follow predictable patterns (like Q3Sales2024!, then Q4Sales2024!, or "Hulu4me!" and "Netflix4me!"). The problem is that, if one of those accounts gets breached, hackers can and will use that pattern to break into everything else.

A good password manager eliminates that excuse. It generates unique, strong passwords for every system **without relying on your memory**. And, when you do this, there's nothing to pattern-match.

All it takes is one reused password for an attacker to breach multiple systems. Don't let that be your weak link.

Security Is a Culture, Not a Checkbox

Installing antivirus software and enforcing MFA are great, but they're not the finish line. Real security requires people who are *thinking* about threats. It's not a task you check off — it's a mindset you build into your team.

What Culture Looks Like in Practice

- Employees question suspicious emails instead of clicking them.
- Staff report possible phishing messages without shame or hesitation.
- IT processes are written down, revisited, and followed.

♦ Tools are used consistently, not just installed and forgotten.

Trust But Confirm

Train your team to verify any unusual request using a different communication channel.

♦ If you get a weird email, call the sender using a known number.

♦ If someone texts you asking to wire money, confirm with a phone call.

♦ Never trust phone numbers or links *within* a suspicious message

Some teams even use **verbal passwords**, which are pre-agreed phrases that verify authenticity when confirming something by phone or text.

It's not about paranoia — it's about *preparedness*. Build a culture where skepticism is healthy and verification is automatic.

Case Stories: When Security Scales, So Does Confidence

These stories illustrate how even the best tools can fall short without proper habits — and how small businesses can punch above their weight when security becomes part of their culture.

Consulting Firm: Skipped MFA, Full Breach

Background: A six-person business consulting firm used Microsoft 365 but had not yet enforced MFA across all users. One partner insisted that MFA was inconvenient and opted out. Everyone else followed suit.

The Problem: That same partner reused a password that had already been exposed in a previous data breach. Their account was compromised, and the attacker used it to send malicious attachments to several clients before anyone noticed.

The Fix: The breach cost them two clients and caused serious reputational harm. They brought in an IT provider to lock down accounts, enforce MFA, implement a password manager, and add IRONSCALES — something they hadn't used before — which would have caught and stopped the phishing attempt earlier.

The Outcome: No additional incidents occurred, but the damage was done. Staff became security-conscious but only after the fact.

Lesson Learned: If one person can bypass security, the whole business is at risk. Security policies only work if they're universal.

Engineering Firm: Security That Runs Itself

Background: A 10-person mechanical engineering firm onboarded with an MSP that set up LastPass for Business, enforced MFA, deployed SentinelOne for EDR, and rolled out IRONSCALES organization-wide.

The Problem: A phishing email bypassed their email filter and hit several inboxes. One staff member reported it, and IRONSCALES automatically removed it from the rest of the team's inboxes within minutes.

The Fix: Because the business had invested in the right stack — and trained their people to report threats — the attack was stopped with zero impact.

The Outcome: The firm didn't just avoid disaster — they used the event as a training opportunity and a proof point that their systems worked.

Lesson Learned: Great security isn't loud. It's invisible until it saves you. Culture, tools, and automation working together make security scalable.

The TL;DR

- **MFA is nonnegotiable.** It's still one of the best protections against account compromise.

- **Antivirus software isn't enough.** Upgrade to EDR tools that detect suspicious behavior, especially on Mac devices.

- **Email is still the #1 way bad guys get in.** Train your team, use smart filtering, and never treat email security as "done."

- **Passwords aren't personal anymore.** Use a password manager with team vaults, offboarding workflows, and enforcement.

- **Security is a habit, not a tool.** Build a culture of skepticism, verification, and ongoing awareness.

- **Security that scales isn't about buying the fanciest tools.** It's about building consistent habits that protect your people and your business every day.

Security isn't just about firewalls and filters. It's also about who has access to what and when.

In the next chapter, we'll break down how to manage user access properly, reduce risk during offboarding, and finally clean up that shared login spreadsheet.

CHAPTER 7

User Access and Risk Management

Rethinking Access

Let's imagine your business as a building. You've got front doors (email), internal hallways (file access), and locked rooms (sensitive client data). Now, imagine giving everyone — your assistant, your contractor, that intern from two summers ago — **a master key**. That's what poor user access looks like.

Access control isn't about mistrusting your team. It's about protecting your business from accidents, mistakes, and worst-case scenarios.

In this chapter, we'll talk about who should have access to what, how long they should have it, and how to take it away without breaking everything.

Common-Sense Access: Trust with Boundaries

You'll hear IT people talk about the principle of "least privilege," which means people should only have access to what they need to do their job — and no more.

Think of it like a restaurant kitchen:

♦ The dishwasher doesn't need the safe code.

♦ The chef doesn't need access to payroll.

♦ The manager has broader access but still not everything.

Now, here's the important nuance: **You can implement least privilege and still have full trust and confidence in your staff.** This isn't about suspicion. It's about protection, consistency, and smart operations. Mistakes happen. Roles change. You're simply limiting exposure to reduce risk, not making a statement about someone's character.

It might feel silly to create a role like "Marketing" or "Admin" and assign it to the one person who does that job. But do it anyway. Role-based permissions are worth it, even if you only have one person in each role today.

Why? Because when someone gets promoted or shifts responsibilities, or you bring in a new hire, you already know what they need access to. You're not scrambling to figure it out — or worse, overprovisioning just to avoid the hassle. **You're scaling with intention.**

Here's a human-friendly way to apply the principle of "least privilege":

♦ If someone doesn't *actively need* access to something, don't give it "just in case."

♦ Use *role-based permissions* wherever possible (even for solo roles).

♦ Review permissions regularly — especially after role changes or team departures.

Shared Logins Are a Security Nightmare

If your whole team is logging into a service using the same username and password, you've got a problem. And, according to a study by Carnegie Mellon, employees share credentials for an average of 11 accounts with coworkers.[14] That's not collaboration — it's a security minefield.

Why shared logins are a bad idea:

♦ You can't track who did what.

♦ You can't revoke access without locking everyone out.

♦ If that password leaks, *everyone* is exposed.

♦ It often violates the terms of service for many platforms.

The fix? Individual accounts under a shared business plan. Yes, it might cost a little more — but it pays off in accountability, traceability, and easier onboarding and offboarding.

Offboarding Is Where Most Breaches Begin

When someone leaves your team — especially under stressful or messy circumstances — you need to act fast. Lingering access is one of the most common causes of breaches in small businesses. Shockingly, 36% of former employees still have active access to company systems after they've left.[15] If you're not automatically deprovisioning accounts, you're gambling with your data.

Here's what proper offboarding looks like:

♦ Immediately disable their email and password manager accounts.

- ◆ Revoke access to shared folders, CRMs, and internal tools.
- ◆ Change passwords for any accounts they had direct login access to.
- ◆ Use an IT-managed "offboarding checklist" to make sure nothing slips through.

If you've followed the advice in earlier chapters (Chapter 2. "Centralization (and Consolidation) Are Critical" and Chapter 6. "Security That Scales"), this process is much simpler. If not, it's time-consuming and risky. It can make the difference between a 10-minute task and a 10-hour nightmare.

Temporary Access Should Be … Temporary

How many tools or documents do you still have shared with a freelancer or ex-employee from two years ago?

Always give time-bound access when possible. Many platforms now allow you to:

- ◆ Set auto-expiration on shared links.
- ◆ Grant temporary, project-specific access.
- ◆ See an audit trail of access and file activity.

If your platform doesn't support these features, keep a manual list of temporary users and review it annually or even quarterly.

Shared Drives and Shared Sites Done Right

Centralized access starts with a centralized structure.

Rather than having one giant company folder with a tangle of subfolder permissions (where nobody's really sure who can see what), use Shared Drives in Google Workspace or Sites in Microsoft SharePoint.

These platforms are built for structured, role-based access management and help avoid permission chaos.

Here's the idea:

♦ Create one shared drive or site per department or function (HR, Marketing, Operations).

♦ Set access at the drive/site level, not individual folders within them.

♦ Assign roles like "Viewer," "Contributor," or "Manager" based on job duties.

♦ Avoid storing sensitive business data in someone's personal drive or OneDrive folder.

Why it matters:

♦ It's easier to onboard and offboard team members.

♦ You reduce the risk of inherited permissions or oversharing.

♦ You can control ownership and visibility from one place.

In short, use your platform's built-in sharing architecture as intended. It's not just cleaner — it's safer and far easier to scale.

You Can't Protect What You Don't Know You Have

Finally, make it someone's job (even if it's yours for now) to keep a running list of:

♦ What tools your business uses

♦ Who has access to each one

♦ What data is stored where

This becomes your "access inventory" — an incredibly valuable document when hiring, auditing, or responding to incidents. It's not glamorous, but it's gold.

Case Stories: Access Control Done Right (and Wrong)

These two stories show how role-based access can prevent chaos — and how the lack of it can amplify it.

Law Firm: Too Much Access, Too Much Risk

Background: A law firm with 11 staff members gave every employee access to every system "just in case." Interns had access to client files. Marketing staff had access to HR documents. No one had any idea who could see what.

The Problem: A departing employee, who was frustrated with their exit, downloaded sensitive internal reports and client onboarding data, which violated internal policies and triggered a client complaint.

The Fix: Their IT vendor overhauled the firm's permissions using a role-based model — Finance, Operations, Marketing, and Admin — and each had clearly defined access levels. Google Shared Drives replaced ad hoc folder sharing.

The Outcome: No further incidents. Onboarding and offboarding became easier. Confidence in internal systems went up, especially among leadership.

Lesson Learned: Over-access isn't convenient — it's dangerous. Most people don't need access to everything, and limiting access helps *everyone*.

Engineering Consulting Group: Roles from Day One

Background: A five-person engineering consulting group decided early on to set up role-based access, even when there was only one person in each role. Their file server, password manager, and project systems were all segmented by function.

The Problem: When their first project manager left the company, they realized how smoothly everything transitioned. Access was turned off in minutes. No scrambling. No forgotten passwords or shared logins. It was … uneventful.

The Fix: The incoming project manager was onboarded in under an hour using the same templates. They just inherited the role, and the role had all the right access baked in.

The Outcome: That system scaled as they grew to 13 people. Their IT vendor simply added new hires into their roles and fine-tuned from there.

Lesson Learned: Role-based access isn't overkill for small teams. It's the secret to seamless scaling — and sleeping better at night.

The TL;DR

- Follow the principle of "least privilege." Give people access only to what they actively need, even if you trust them completely.

- Avoid shared logins. Use individual accounts tied to business roles to improve security and accountability.

- Offboard quickly and thoroughly. Disable access and rotate passwords immediately.

- Temporary access should have an expiration date. Review and clean it up regularly.

- Use Shared Drives (Google) or Sites (SharePoint) for centralized, role-based file management. Don't bury permissions in messy subfolders.

- Keep an access inventory including what tools you use, who has access, and where data lives.

You've locked down access and improved your security posture. Now it's time to focus on how your team actually works within those systems.

Next up: workflows that scale, templates that save time, and naming conventions that keep things running smoothly.

CHAPTER 8

Build Workflows That Scale with You

Why Workflow Matters

Let's start with a hard truth: Most small business workflows are duct tape and hope.

You build something that "works for now" and keep piling tools and tasks on top of it until it breaks — or until you're spending more time managing your process than doing your actual work.

Here's the thing: Proper workflows aren't just a nice-to-have: Workers overwhelmingly believe it reduces wasted time (69%), cuts down on human error (66%), and frees them from repetitive tasks (59%).[16] Smart workflows can amplify your team's effectiveness without adding headcount.

This chapter is about helping you step back, look at the bigger picture, and start building workflows that can grow with you — not fight against you.

Let Your Process Define Your Tools

Too many businesses start by picking a tool — and then force their process to fit it. That's backwards.

Instead, map out how your business actually runs and ask these questions:

- How do clients come in?
- What steps happen after a sale?
- Who does what and when?
- What gets delivered and how?

Once these questions are answered, find tools that support those steps, not dictate them. Your tech should mold around your workflow, not the other way around.

The Power of Consistent Folder Structures and Naming

It sounds small, but standardizing your file and folder setup is a game-changer. Why?

- You reduce friction when collaborating.
- You make onboarding new staff or contractors way easier.
- You avoid "Where did I save that?" syndrome.

Create a folder hierarchy that mirrors your process. For example:

Clients/

    — 2024/

        — Smith_Legal/

            — Intake

                — Contracts

                    — Deliverables

Pair that with clear file-naming conventions ("2024-04_Smith_Contract_FINAL.pdf"). You'll be shocked at how much time and stress it saves.

PRO TIP

Less is more. If you adopt a strong naming convention, like beginning each file name with a YYYY-MM-DD format, you may not need to separate documents into year-based folders at all. The naming structure makes it easy to sort and find files chronologically, which helps you avoid overorganizing and reduces unnecessary folder sprawl. •

Templates Are a Secret Weapon

Every time you reuse an old document or email, you're halfway to a template.

Make it official:

♦ Intake forms

♦ Onboarding checklists

♦ Recurring client emails

♦ Monthly reports

Turn them into Google Docs, Microsoft Word templates, or form-based automations. Bonus points if you connect them to your CRM or file system.

Don't Reinvent the Wheel — Steal from Yourself

One of the most overlooked benefits of good workflows is **reuse**. You've probably already solved 80% of the problems you're facing. But you just don't have a system for repeating that solution consistently.

Every time you ...

♦ customize a proposal

♦ deliver a finished product

♦ send a follow-up email

♦ complete a new hire onboarding

... you're creating a template-in-waiting. Instead of starting from scratch each time, **build a bank of reusable assets** — and make sure your team knows where to find them.

What to save:

♦ Client email sequences (in a shared doc or CRM template library)

♦ Proposal formats

♦ Onboarding checklists

♦ Task-list templates in your project management tool

You'll save hours, reduce errors, and create consistency that scales.

Automate the Busywork with Intentionality

Automation can be magical — or a mess. The key is to automate the boring, repeatable stuff — not the complex, judgment-heavy steps.

Despite its clear benefits, only 31% of businesses have automated even a single function.[17] That's a huge opportunity for small companies to leap ahead with lean, efficient workflows that scale without chaos.

And, on that note, here are some good automation targets:

♦ New client intake notifications

♦ Appointment scheduling (Calendly, Microsoft Bookings)

♦ Document routing and filing

◆ Payment confirmations and invoice reminders

Start small. One well-placed automation can save you hours each month.

Document Your Process Now, Not Later

You'll never feel like you have time to document how your business runs. That's why so few do it. Then, when they're trying to train someone or hand off a task, they realize *nothing is written down*.

Start simple:

◆ Record a Loom video while walking through a task.

◆ List the steps in a shared doc.

◆ Create a "How We Work" folder.

It doesn't need to be perfect — it just needs to exist. Bonus points? Nothing helps someone learn a process quite like trying to explain it to someone else.

Once you have an initial version of a documented process, delegate the completion of that documentation to the person who needs to learn that process most!

Automate First, Delegate Second, Do Last

When it comes to managing repetitive tasks in your business, there's a smart order of operations. This isn't about being lazy. It's about using your time (and your team's time) in the most efficient, scalable way possible. This hierarchy makes your workflow more efficient and keeps you focused on work that actually moves your business forward.

Step 1. Automate

If the task is repetitive, predictable, and happens on a schedule or trigger, automate it. Whether it's sending an email when a form is filled out, filing a document in the right folder, or logging a payment into your CRM, well-placed automation can quietly remove hours of work every week.

Step 2. Delegate

If the task can't be automated — or not yet — your next option is to delegate. But don't just dump tasks onto someone else. You need to set them up for success. Make sure you have a clear, repeatable process, and document it once, so you don't have to repeat yourself 10 times later.

Step 3. Do It Yourself

Doing tasks manually should be the last resort, not the default. If you're still manually sending calendar invites, digging up documents, or chasing status updates, it's time to revisit Steps 1 and 2. You may think it takes less time to just DIY really quickly, and you may be right — if it is just once. But if it continues to come up over time, it's essential to not have it sap you of your precious time.

Don't Take It Too Far

If you have ADHD or are otherwise on the spectrum (Hey, that's me!), you may be tempted to take this management issue to as much of an extreme as you can. But remember the golden rule: everything in moderation.

xkcd has a great infographic on their website illustrating how much time you save vs. spend while attempting to automate something.[18]

Remember: You can spend so much time trying to free up time that you ... well ... lose too much time doing it.

(Oh, and on the topic of ADHD and the spectrum, I have a running theory that a disproportionately higher number of small business owners are on the spectrum and/or have ADHD specifically compared to the general population. It mirrors my lived experience. I can see how we would naturally gravitate towards running a business when we analyze how many hats we end up wearing. Please note that I have absolutely no statistics to support this theory — but it's fun to think about!)

Case Stories: Simplicity, Naming, and Workflow That Works

These stories highlight how the little things — file naming, folder structure, repeatable workflows — can make or break a growing business.

Law Firm: Naming Conventions That Prevented Chaos

Background: A four-person law firm stored all files in a shared Dropbox account. Folders were created ad hoc, often named inconsistently ("Smith-Johnson Docs," "JS Contract v2," and "2023 Client"), with no clear version control.

The Problem: During a discovery request, two paralegals spent three days trying to find the latest signed contract for a client. Multiple drafts were saved in different folders with similar names. No one had confidence when looking for the final version.

The Fix: They migrated to Box for compliance and security reasons and implemented a naming convention using date-based formatting

(YYYY-MM-DD) and version control suffixes (v1, v2, FINAL). Each matter had its own standardized folder template.

The Outcome: The next time a court filing came due, it took under two minutes to retrieve the correct document. Time was saved, and confidence soared.

Lesson Learned: If you can't find it, you can't use it. Naming conventions are like signage in your digital office. Don't run your firm without them.

Engineering Firm: From Folder Soup to Flow

Background: An eight-person civil engineering firm had grown fast. Every project manager had their own way of organizing files — some used years, some used project codes, and some just dumped everything into a catch-all folder called "Active Projects."

The Problem: Staff couldn't onboard new team members effectively. One new hire accidentally duplicated an entire project folder — thinking they were working in a test copy — because there was no clarity regarding which folder was the original.

The Fix: Their IT provider built a company-wide folder structure and template for all new projects. Each one used a consistent naming format and role-based access for engineering, project management, and admin staff.

The Outcome: The firm gained back dozens of hours a month in rework, duplication, and communication breakdown. Staff turnover no longer meant a training nightmare.

Lesson Learned: Workflow isn't just about speed — it's about clarity. When everyone follows the same map, nobody gets lost.

The TL;DR

- Design your workflow first and then choose tools to support it — not the other way around.

- Standardize folders and file names to cut confusion and save time.

- Use templates wherever you can. If you do something twice, template it.

- Automate the repeatable stuff and not the judgment calls.

- Start documenting your process now. It only gets harder the longer you wait.

Once your processes are dialed in, the tools you choose can either amplify your results or create more problems.

In the next chapter, I'll help you pick the right SaaS tools for a small business and highlight what to avoid as you build your tech toolkit.

PART III

Tools That Work for You (Not Against You)

CHAPTER 9

SaaS That Works for the 1-20 Crowd

SaaS for the 99%

Let's talk software.

Not the bloated, 500-seat enterprise kind. Buying the biggest or most feature-rich SaaS tool sounds smart until you realize you're only using a fraction of what you're paying for. In fact, 53% of SaaS licenses go unused or underutilized, leading to massive waste in software spend.[19]

And we're not fans of the "built in a basement and hasn't been updated since 2014" kind either. (More on that in "Core Categories to Get Right" in this chapter.)

This chapter is about SaaS platforms that work *right now* for the **1- to 20-person business** — scalable, secure, affordable, and actually helpful. Whether you're solo or growing, you need tools that won't fight you on price, complexity, or flexibility.

What "Best in Class" Really Means at Your Size

You don't need the same tech stack as Salesforce or Deloitte. But that doesn't mean you should settle for second-rate or "custom-built" tools either.

The sweet spot:

♦ Simple enough to use without an IT department

♦ Powerful enough to grow with you

♦ Secure enough to pass a client audit

♦ Affordable enough to scale without regret

This chapter breaks down **smart picks** across different categories and highlights tools you should absolutely **avoid** — no matter how tempting they seem.

Core Categories to Get Right

Here are the categories where your choices really matter:

Email + Productivity Suite

♦ **Google Workspace:** Ideal for simplicity, real-time collaboration, and ease of onboarding; great if your business relies heavily on Google Docs, Sheets, or Calendar

♦ **Microsoft 365:** Best if you need granular control over licensing costs, have HIPAA or FINRA compliance requirements, or if you (or your staff) require Outlook as your default email/calendar platform

Whichever you choose, commit to it and configure it properly. If you're finding your needs split — say, you love Google Calendar but need to use Microsoft Outlook for whatever reason (there is a very small list for why you'd need Outlook, but that's another story) — you'll need to prioritize which platform matters more to your workflow. In cases where both are critical, you may want to work with an IT provider to manage a hybrid environment.

There's nuance here, and hybrid setups should only be approached on a case-by-case basis with expert input. (See "Hybrid Environments Are a Trap" in Chapter 2. "Centralization (and Consolidation) Are Critical" for more info.)

File Storage

♦ **Box:** Especially good for firms that need HIPAA, FINRA, or other compliance-level storage; solid version control and user management

♦ **SharePoint (via Microsoft 365):** Great for internal document libraries and intranet-style structure

♦ **Google Drive (via Google Workspace):** Great for small teams with a simple folder structure and strong search needs

Avoid Dropbox. It's not a backup tool, and its admin controls are too weak for growing businesses. Worse, there are very few tools that can properly back up Dropbox data. Most enterprise-grade backup platforms built for Google Workspace and Microsoft 365 simply don't support it. Dropbox is still mostly considered a consumer-grade tool, and it doesn't offer anything you can't already get (and secure) through a single set of Google or Microsoft accounts — without the extra cost and complexity. (See "Why Dropbox Is Not a Backup Tool" in Chapter 3. "Back Up Before You Blackout.")

Password Management

- **1Password, LastPass for Business, or Dashlane for Business:** All are solid. Just pick one and use it consistently.

CRM

- **HubSpot (Free or Starter tiers):** Good for general small-biz use, lightweight, and easy to adopt
- **Clio:** Built for law firms. Includes billing, case management, and document storage
- **Redtail:** Designed for financial professionals. FINRA-compliant, and tailored to client advisory work

If you don't have a CRM, start with something basic. Even a good shared spreadsheet is better than keeping client notes in your head.

Integrations Are a Superpower

Modern SaaS tools should **talk to each other**. If your email, calendar, invoicing, and project management tools are disconnected, you're doubling your workload.

Look for:

- **Native integrations** (built-in connections between tools)
- Zapier or Make.com compatibility (for custom automations)
- **API access** (if you plan to work with a software and/or website developer or advanced IT provider, see "Beware of Custom Apps" in this chapter for warnings on this approach)

Even small automations (like creating a folder when a deal is won in your CRM) can save huge amounts of time at scale.

Beware of Custom Apps

Custom software can sound appealing with tailored features, total control, and maybe even a local developer who says they can build exactly what you want. But, for most small businesses, **custom apps are a trap**.

Here's why:

♦ They're nearly impossible to maintain without the original developer.

♦ Updates, fixes, and compatibility changes become expensive and slow.

♦ They rarely integrate cleanly with your other tools, making everything feel clunky.

You end up spending way too much time (and therefore money) chasing bugs or rebuilding features that already exist in mature platforms.

Unless software is your business, don't try to build your own. You're better off adjusting your process slightly to fit a solid SaaS tool than building something fragile and one-off from scratch.

Don't Buy a Tool for Just One Client

This one's important.

Every now and then, a big client asks you to adopt a specific platform to work with them. Unless you're billing enough to justify the overhead, **don't do it**.

You need a stack that works for *your* operations, not a patchwork of client-requested tools. In some cases, it's fine to meet them halfway, but your business infrastructure needs to be *yours*.

Case Stories: Choosing SaaS Tools That Actually Work

These stories illustrate what happens when software selection is driven by short-term convenience versus long-term scalability, and how smart, centralized tools unlock growth.

Financial Advisory Firm: Custom CRM, Constant Frustration

Background: A 10-person financial advisory firm commissioned a custom-built CRM solution to match their exact client workflow. At first, it seemed like a good investment.

The Problem: A year later, the original developers stopped supporting it. No one internally knew how it worked under the hood. Every feature update or bug fix required a costly contract with a new dev shop, and integrations with email and calendars never worked right.

The Fix: The firm transitioned to Redtail, a CRM built specifically for financial services. With their IT provider's help, they migrated client data, synced email/calendar integration, and trained the team on workflows.

The Outcome: The firm now runs leaner, with real-time access to the data they need. Their software is maintained by a real company, and their IT partner can support it without coding knowledge.

Lesson Learned: Custom software may solve today's pain, but off-the-shelf platforms with industry backing scale further, faster, and with far fewer headaches.

Engineering Firm: From Disconnected Apps to a True Stack

Background: A six-person mechanical engineering team used Microsoft 365 for email, Google Calendar for scheduling, Dropbox for file sharing, and Zoom for meetings. Passwords were stored in browser autofill or personal notes.

The Problem: Nothing connected. Calendar invites didn't sync. File permissions were unclear. Passwords were forgotten or shared informally. During a key client presentation, they couldn't open the correct document live because it was in the wrong Dropbox account.

The Fix: Their IT provider unified their systems under Microsoft 365. They implemented SharePoint for file sharing, Outlook for calendars, Teams for meetings, and Dashlane for Business to manage passwords across staff.

The Outcome: The team didn't just reduce friction — they gained a tech backbone that could scale with them. New hires had clear onboarding, and client meetings ran without a hitch.

Lesson Learned: You don't need fewer tools — you need better-connected ones. When your stack is designed to work together, your team does too.

The TL;DR

- ◆ Choose SaaS tools designed for 1-20 person teams. Look for simplicity, scalability, and strong security.
- ◆ Google Workspace is best if you rely on Docs, Sheets, or Calendar. Microsoft 365 is ideal for Outlook users or if you need HIPAA/FINRA compliance.

- Avoid hybrid platforms unless you have expert IT support — prioritize your most critical workflows.

- Use Box, SharePoint, or Google Drive for storage — not Dropbox. Dropbox lacks proper admin tools and isn't easily backed up.

- A business-grade password manager is essential. Pick one and deploy it across your team.

- Start with a basic CRM: Clio for legal, Redtail for finance, or HubSpot for general use.

- Favor tools that integrate with each other and support automation. Manual work doesn't scale.

- Custom-built apps are risky, expensive, and fragile. Stick to supported platforms unless software *is* your business.

- Don't let clients dictate your tech stack. Build for your needs first — don't overbuy or oversimplify.

With the right tools in place, it's easy to feel invincible. But every business faces disruptions sooner or later. The real question is whether you're prepared.

Coming up: how to plan for worst-case scenarios, so your business can keep moving forward.

CHAPTER 10

Plan for the Worst (So You Can Stay at Your Best)

Not If, But When

Hope isn't a plan, and failing to plan is planning to fail. In any business, **things will go wrong**: power outages, internet outages, SaaS tool outages, data breaches, ransomware attacks, natural disasters, human error ... the list goes on and on. It's not a matter of *if*, it's a matter of *when*.

The good news? You don't need to turn into a doomsday prepper. But you *do* need a plan.

This chapter is all about **disaster recovery and business continuity** — two boring-sounding terms that just mean, "How do we react, survive, and get back up and running when everything hits the fan?"

Disaster Recovery vs. Business Continuity: What's the Difference?

♦ **Disaster recovery:** How you get your systems and data back after something breaks; the technical fix of restoring backups, replacing hardware, and bringing systems back online

♦ **Business continuity:** How you keep serving clients *while* that recovery is happening; about the processes, communication, and temporary workflows that keep the lights on in the meantime

Disaster recovery focuses on **systems**. Business continuity focuses on **people and process**. If you only plan for one, you're still exposed, and panicked leaders are not good leaders.

Let's say your cloud storage is encrypted by ransomware. Disaster recovery gets your files back from backup. But business continuity is what gets your team paid, your clients updated, and your emails answered while that happens.

You need both. Backups are part of it, sure (see Chapter 3. "Back Up Before You Blackout"). But equally important are **procedures, people, communication, and your cyber liability insurance**. Yes, that's part of business continuity too. If a breach or major outage occurs, one of your first calls should be to your insurance provider to begin the claims process. You *do* have a cyber liability policy, right? If not, go back and reread Chapter 4. "Cyber Liability Insurance: Your Financial Firewall."

Start with These Questions

♦ **What are the systems you can't function without?** This is your business' heartbeat: email, calendars, client documents, billing tools, and scheduling apps. These are the things that, if

CHAPTER 10. PLAN FOR THE WORST
(SO YOU CAN STAY AT YOUR BEST)

they went offline, would immediately grind your operations to a halt. Identify them early, so you know what to prioritize in a crisis.

♦ **How fast do you need these systems back online?** If your email goes down, can you survive for a few hours, or does it need to be back within 15 minutes? Not everything has the same urgency. Rank your tools by how quickly they need to be recovered to keep your business afloat.

♦ **Who's responsible for what when things go sideways?** When chaos hits, you want clarity — not confusion. Who makes the call to notify clients? Who starts restoring systems? Who is talking to your IT provider or insurance carrier? These tasks shouldn't all fall on one person's shoulders. Having a clear delegation of roles turns panic into a checklist ... and that's a powerful shift.

Create a "Business Down" Checklist

This checklist doesn't have to be a 40-page binder. Start with a single-page plan:

♦ What should the team do if they can't access key systems?

♦ Who needs to be contacted (staff, clients, and vendors)?

♦ How do you communicate the issue externally without causing panic?

♦ What are the fallback tools or processes?

♦ Who is responsible for which steps within the checklist?

This plan should live in a secure, **offline-accessible location**, like a printed page or password-protected file stored outside your main system. (After all, this is for emergencies like abruptly losing an internet connection or losing access to all of your business files. If you rely on your primary systems to store your emergency checklist … well, you'll be in for a rude shock when you actually need to use it.)

Write It Down — But It Matters More to Test

You can have the prettiest plan in the world, but if no one's ever run through it, it's almost useless. Similarly, writing a DRP is a solid start. But, if you're not testing it, it's just fiction. Shockingly, 23% of companies never test their DR plans at all,[20] which means they're betting on a strategy that may not work when it counts.

Once a year (or after a big team change), do a **dry run**:

♦ Simulate a system outage.

♦ Walk through your plan.

♦ Fix the things that break during testing.

Think of it like a fire drill for your business. Yes, it's a hassle. But, when a real fire hits, you'll be glad you practiced. Time is everything when you're down. According to Veeam, the average total recovery time after a ransomware attack is 3.4 weeks.[21] You could get *partially* up and running much sooner than this, but before you're back to 100%? That's nearly a month of disrupted business — assuming you're able to recover at all.

When to Involve Your IT Provider

If you've outsourced IT — or plan to — make sure they're looped into your continuity plan **before** something goes wrong. Your IT provider should be an active participant in building, testing, and executing your disaster recovery strategy. Not someone you call in a panic with no context. *I cannot stress this enough.*

Here are the questions you should ask your IT partner ahead of time:

CHAPTER 10. PLAN FOR THE WORST
(SO YOU CAN STAY AT YOUR BEST)

- What happens if *you* (the business owner) are unavailable in a crisis? Who is the secondary point of contact who has authority to make fast decisions in your absence?

- Who has admin access and/or permission to restore critical systems?

- What is their response time guarantee? Check your SLA for major outages.

- Can they walk you through how they'd recover your most important services?

- Do they maintain documentation or logs of your infrastructure?

- Have they tested restoring a backup *recently*?

You're not just looking for technical answers. You're looking for confidence, clarity, and readiness. If they can't give you a straight answer — or if they start asking you why this is needed or tell you this is overkill — **they're not the right partner**.

Disaster planning is a team sport. Your IT provider should know the playbook, not be reading it for the first time on game day.

Case Stories: Business Continuity in Real Life

This chapter brings to life what continuity actually means in practice — not just backups but keeping the business running in the face of disruption.

Law Firm: Cloud Saved the Court Date

Background: A small but busy law firm of five handled everything on local desktop computers in the office. Their case management software was also locally hosted.

The Problem: The office experienced a sudden power outage due to a transformer failure the morning of a scheduled court appearance. Their lead attorney had no access to the necessary documents, which were saved on their office desktop.

The Fix: After the incident, the firm transitioned to a cloud-based practice management solution (Clio), migrated files to Box, and shifted to laptops with VPN access to ensure continuity in emergencies.

The Outcome: Weeks later, when a similar outage occurred, the attorney calmly accessed the court file from home and made their appearance on time without any last-minute panic.

Lesson Learned: Downtime doesn't just cost money — it can cost outcomes. Business continuity means access anywhere, anytime.

Engineering Firm: When the Flood Came

Background: An 18-person engineering firm operated from a single office location with an NAS system for all project files.

The Problem: A pipe burst over a holiday weekend, flooding the office and destroying the NAS. No offsite backup existed. It took five days just to access partial copies of project files from old email threads and months to rebuild what was lost.

The Fix: They brought in an IT company to rebuild their infrastructure using cloud-first systems, implemented Spanning for automated backup, and trained the staff on disaster protocol.

The Outcome: They now run hybrid with Google Workspace and Box, and all project data is redundantly backed up. They're also insured for data loss under their cyber liability policy.

Lesson Learned: You can't predict disasters, but you can prepare for them. Business continuity is about planning for "when," not "if."

The TL;DR

♦ Bad things happen. Planning beats panicking.

♦ Disaster recovery = getting systems back. Business continuity = staying functional in the meantime.

♦ Make a simple, written plan covering contacts, priorities, and actions.

♦ Use the 3-2-1 backup rule: 3 copies, 2 formats, 1 offsite.

♦ Test your plan at least once a year before you actually need it.

♦ Include your IT provider in your disaster recovery strategy.

Disaster recovery is critical, but so is your everyday setup. Now let's talk about hardware.

In the next chapter, I'll show you how to budget for equipment, avoid costly surprises, and know when it's time to replace aging machines.

PART IV

Growth Building

CHAPTER 11

Your Machines Age: Know How to Budget and When to Upgrade

Why Hardware Still Matters in a Cloud-Centric World

Cloud-based apps and storage have changed the game, but that doesn't mean your physical gear is suddenly irrelevant. On the contrary: Your laptops, desktops, phones, and tablets are still the bridge between your team and the cloud. And, if that bridge is slow, underpowered, or breaking down, everything suffers.

Even when your data lives in the cloud, **device specs still matter**. An employee trying to run video calls, manage cloud-based documents, and handle a few dozen browser tabs on a laptop with 4GB of RAM and a tiny hard drive is going to struggle. *A lot.*

Don't let the "we're cloud-first" mindset fool you. Your devices still need to be fast, secure, and reliable.

BYOD vs. Company-Owned: Choose Your Adventure (Wisely)

Let's talk ownership. Should your team bring their own laptops, or should you provide company computers?

RULE OF THUMB

- If the person is a **W-2 employee**, issue a business-grade laptop or desktop.
- If they're a **1099 contractor**, BYOD *might* be acceptable. But, even then, I would be cautious about making such a cut-and-dried separation. ●

The real issue comes down to control. **You can only enforce security, backups, and acceptable-use policies on business-owned devices.** If someone is using their personal laptop, you're trusting them to keep software up to date, run antivirus software, avoid storing sensitive info locally, and follow best practices on their own. You *can* load these tools on their personal machines — but only if they consent to it. That's a big gamble, especially in regulated industries or client-service businesses.

Defaulting to BYOD might seem like a budget win, but it often turns into a security and support headache. And if you're regulated? A security headache could quickly become a financial one if a personal device isn't up to code and you end up violating HIPAA or FINRA. Choose wisely.

Partial BYOD: Company Laptops and Personal Phones

Another common variation I've seen over the years is more of a "partial" BYOD policy. In these cases, small businesses strike a middle ground by **issuing company-owned computers** but allowing team members to use their **personal smartphones or tablets** for email, messaging, or MFA apps. This hybrid approach can work, but only if it's handled intentionally.

While laptops can be tightly managed with MDM and security tools, **mobile BYOD introduces gray areas**. You'll want to add clear policies and MDM solutions like Microsoft Intune or Google Workspace's endpoint management to enforce things like:

♦ Screen lock and encryption

♦ Remote wipe for lost/stolen devices

♦ App restrictions and containerization (especially for email or document access)

Also consider what happens if someone leaves. Can you selectively wipe business data off their phone without touching their photos or texts? A partial BYOD policy offers flexibility. But, like any compromise, it requires planning to avoid creating hidden vulnerabilities. As with any BYOD policy, there is also the issue of employee/contractor consent (see "Monitoring: What's Legal, What's Practical, What's Ethical" in Chapter 15. "Where HR Meets IT: Security, Monitoring, and Onboarding" for additional HR considerations).

The Silent Budget Killer: Random, Reactive Buying

Most small businesses buy computers when someone's computer dies or starts lagging. Panic sets in. A Costco run happens. A box gets opened, and BOOM! Problem solved ... for now.

Where does this stem from? Many small businesses delay upgrading their computers to stretch budgets or prioritize other IT needs. But this strategy backfires, leading to security vulnerabilities, slow performance, and software that no longer plays nice — and then they're always on their back foot when something does go wrong.

But here's the trap: Most people buy what's on the shelf, not what fits their real business needs. The most common spec issue? **Insufficient hard-drive capacity.** A 256GB drive might be fine for a basic admin user with very little data needs. But, if your team handles large files (designs, photos, videos, legal docs), it'll fill up fast. Even "average" case computers fill up very quickly on a 256GB hard drive. Throw in low RAM or not enough ports, and you're looking at early obsolescence, poor performance, and expensive workarounds.

Reactive buying also leads to mismatched equipment, spotty warranties, and ballooning IT costs. It's not a strategy — it's damage control.

Get Organized Before You Buy Anything

Before you buy another device for your business, **get your hardware life in order**. Create a simple asset tracker. It could be a spreadsheet or a more fully featured asset manager like Asset Panda. If you're working with an IT provider, you could also collaborate with them using IT Glue/MyGlue.

Track these fields at minimum:

- Purchase price
- Make/model
- Assigned user
- Date of purchase
- Depreciation schedule

- End-of-life date
- Warranty expiration
- Serial number
- Device specs (RAM, storage, processor)

You can't manage what you don't track. This list will save your bacon when a laptop dies or a phone is lost or stolen, when planning budgets, or when you're onboarding (or offboarding) a staff member.

Depreciation and Lifecycle: Plan for the Inevitable

All hardware ages. Planning for it means you're not surprised when the time comes to replace it.

RULE OF THUMB

- **Laptops:** Three-year lifecycle
- **Desktops:** Four-year lifecycle
- **Mobile devices (phones/tablets):** Two-year lifecycle

These timelines align with statistical performance degradation, manufacturer support windows, and the pace of software updates and their impact on overall system performance and compatibility. Stretching these timelines too far exponentially increases the risk of hardware failures and compatibility issues.

Also, don't replace everything at once. Stagger your purchases, so you don't face a $20,000 surprise refresh in Year Four. A rolling refresh schedule helps you spread out spending and maintain a more consistent experience for your team.

Why does this matter? Because downtime isn't a fluke — it's becoming the norm. In fact, 76% of organizations experienced downtime due to data loss just last year, up 25% from 2021.[22] **And aging hardware and poor planning are often to blame.**

Budget Like a Grown-Up Business

IT hardware is an operational necessity, not an optional expense. Treat it like you treat rent or payroll: Plan for it.

Build a rolling, four-year hardware budget that accounts for:

- New devices
- Accessories (docking stations, chargers, cables, adapters)
- Monitors and peripherals
- Setup costs (labor, software installation, configuration time)

Buying outright gives you ownership. Leasing helps with cash flow and predictable refresh cycles. Financing is somewhere in between. Choose based on your business needs, but budget either way. (In most cases, buying outright is usually best for smaller businesses, but do your due diligence to confirm this.)

Warranties, Support, and Vendor Selection

Business hardware isn't just about what you buy — it's also where and how.

Always match your **warranty to your depreciation schedule**. If your laptop is on a three-year schedule, get a three-year warranty. Simple. If you're planning to extend the life for a specific reason — like a known staffing change or a delay in capital budgets — consider extending the warranty too.

Just be wary of paying for support past the end of the device's useful life. If you wouldn't drive a car after its failed inspection, don't extend coverage on a failing machine.

PRO TIP

Buy from reliable, business-friendly vendors (Dell, Lenovo, Apple, your managed IT provider). Costco and Amazon can work *if* you're spec-savvy. But they shouldn't be your first stop unless you know exactly what you're buying. •

Refurbs, Hand-Me-Downs, and the Right Way to Recycle

Refurbished equipment can be a smart buy — but only if the math works.

RULE OF THUMB

Discount must match or exceed depreciation. If a new desktop depreciates over four years, a one-year-old refurbished unit should cost **at least 25% less** than it would new *because it only has three out of four years left.* If you don't follow this rule, you're — statistically speaking — throwing money down the drain and saving pennies to lose dollars later in early replacement, repairs, or user frustration. •

Update the depreciation schedule based on age at time of purchase. No exceptions.

When retiring devices, make sure you **wipe them properly**. Tools like DBAN (for hard drives) or factory resets with secure erase options (on SSDs) help ensure company data doesn't get into the wrong hands. You can donate, recycle, or — in some cases — sell fully depreciated devices to employees as a perk.

Case Stories: Surprise Costs vs. Budgeted Spend

Law Firm: The $9,000 Surprise Laptop Spend

Background: A 10-person law firm with no structured hardware plan or IT oversight.

The Problem: Following a ransomware scare, the firm panic-purchased laptops from a retail store without evaluating specs or business needs. Most were consumer-grade devices with inadequate storage and memory.

The Fix: Within a year, they had to replace seven of the 10 machines due to poor performance and inability to access files due to maxed-out hard drives.

The Outcome: The firm ended up spending more than double what they would have if they'd planned ahead, and lost hundreds of staff hours due to data transfers and user frustration.

Lesson Learned: Reactive buying leads to costly mistakes. Business-grade devices and thoughtful specs are worth the upfront planning.

Architectural Engineering Firm : Blueprints and Budgets, and How One Architecture Firm Did It Right

Background: An 18-person architectural engineering firm growing steadily with help from a proactive IT partner.

The Problem: They had no clear record of who had what hardware, how old each device was, or when replacements would be needed.

The Fix: Their IT provider helped them conduct a full hardware audit and then log every device in a shared spreadsheet that included make, model, purchase date, depreciation schedule, and warranty info.

The Outcome: With a complete view of their hardware lifecycle, they created a four-year staggered replacement plan. This leveled out IT spending and eliminated budget spikes and last-minute scrambles.

Lesson Learned: Getting organized pays dividends. Tracking assets and planning upgrades prevents chaos and keeps your IT budget predictable.

The TL;DR

- Hardware still matters, even if your data lives in the cloud.
- Specs like RAM and storage directly impact productivity. Don't cheap out.
- BYOD is risky. You can't enforce security policies on personal devices.
- Random Costco runs lead to mismatched gear and wasted money.
- Track every device in a spreadsheet or asset-management tool.
- Depreciate laptops over three years, desktops over four years, and phones over two years.
- Match warranties to depreciation schedules. Don't over insure expired gear.
- Refurbs are okay if you get a steep enough discount and adjust the lifecycle accordingly.

♦ Budget ahead and stagger purchases to avoid big, sudden hits to your cash flow.

You've got your devices under control, but who's managing everything behind the scenes? At some point, handling IT on your own becomes a liability.

Next, I'll look at how to outsource IT the smart way and build a partnership that works for your business.

CHAPTER 12

When (and How) to Outsource IT the Smart Way

Recognizing When You Need Help

At some point, you're going to outgrow DIY IT.

You'll get tired of being the one who resets everyone's passwords. You'll hit a wall where something breaks, and you *don't know how to fix it*. That's your signal: It's time to outsource. Or maybe you'll decide you need cyber liability coverage, and their questionnaire makes it painfully obvious to you all the IT stuff you don't know but somehow still need to take care of just to get coverage.

But outsourcing your IT isn't just about finding "a computer person." If that's your plan, then you're still stuck in the 2010s. It's about bringing in a **strategic partner** who can help your business grow, stay secure, recover when things go wrong, and *prevent things that can go wrong before they do*.

This chapter is all about recognizing when you need help, how to vet the right provider, and how to set up a relationship that *actually* works.

The IT Outsourcing Continuum

Before we dive into the nitty-gritty of IT providers, let's step back and look at the bigger picture: namely, **how small businesses can actually structure IT support over time**. There's no one-size-fits-all approach. Instead, what we often see is a natural evolution — a continuum, if you will — of IT models based on size, complexity, and business maturity.

While these combinations may vary, most small businesses lean toward fully outsourced IT. Hiring a full-time internal IT person is usually cost-prohibitive until the business is quite large — certainly much larger than the businesses who this book is written for. But understanding your options helps you plan where you are *and* where you want to end up.

The Continuum of IT Support Models

♦ **Reactive IT Support (Hourly IT Consultant):** Most basic model used by very small businesses or solopreneurs. You call an IT person only when something breaks (printer down, can't access email, virus alert). This is typically referred to as a "Break/Fix" model. No monitoring, no ongoing updates, and no proactive support.

  ♦ **Pros:** Low cost, pay-as-you-go. No ongoing contract.

  ♦ **Cons:** No prevention, slow response times, and a tendency to put out fires instead of solving root issues. Often due to lack of preventative infrastructure, more survival-threatening events occur. I tend to nickname this approach "Playing With Fire."

- **Fully Outsourced and Managed IT:** Most common setup for small businesses. You contract with an MSP who handles your monitoring, maintenance, backups, security, and day-to-day troubleshooting.

  - **Pros:** Predictable pricing, 24/7 support options, and access to specialized expertise.

  - **Cons:** Can feel impersonal if too much automation happens on the IT side. Communication and follow-through can vary by provider, and some MSPs may struggle to properly support businesses with less than a staff of 10.

- **Co-Managed IT:** A hybrid model. You engage an MSP for proactive support (monitoring, patching, backups) while also hiring an external IT consultant for hourly support and issue resolution. The MSP handles the baseline while the consultant acts as your on-call tech or project lead.

  - **Pros:** Versatility and vendor flexibility. If you're unhappy with one party, you can swap them out without redoing your whole stack.

  - **Cons:** Communication pitfalls. Two different vendors touching your systems can create confusion, finger-pointing, or duplicated work if expectations aren't crystal clear.

- **In-House IT with Outsourced Support:** Typically happens once you hit 40-100 employees. (So, if you're interested in this model and you're reading this book, chances are you have a way to go before this becomes viable.) You hire an internal IT manager or IT director but continue outsourcing specific functions (cybersecurity, help desk, cloud management).

This is great for businesses that need someone internal who "gets the culture" but don't want to build a full IT department.

- ♦ **Pros:** This person is often full time and has few other work obligations to distract them from focusing entirely on your IT infrastructure and gaining deep knowledge and context relevant to your specific business.

- ♦ **Cons:** A single individual makes them mission-critical to your business, and it becomes difficult to handle day-to-day operations or address IT emergencies when they are on vacation or otherwise become unavailable.

♦ **Fully In-House IT Department:** Rare for businesses under 100 staff. At this point, you likely have an internal CIO, a help desk, a network admin, and cybersecurity personnel. Unless you're in a heavily regulated or tech-intensive industry, this is the far end of the spectrum.

- ♦ **Pros:** A team of IT individuals can cross-train and share many of the advantages of an internal IT manager/director without the same downsides since there is rarely a situation when *all* of them become unavailable at the same time.

- ♦ **Cons:** A fully staffed IT department is expensive, often prohibitively for businesses with 50 or fewer employees, so is not considered very relevant for the scope and purposes of this book and its intended audience.

Each of these models has its own place, and your goal isn't to "level up" through all of them. Your goal is to choose what matches your current needs while staying adaptable. Many small businesses live happily for years in the outsourced or comanaged world.

The key is knowing your setup, managing vendor roles clearly, and revisiting the strategy at least once a year to make sure it still serves your business.

And no, before you ask: I don't include "just do it yourself," "have your assistant set it up," or "get your tech-savvy cousin to help" as viable IT support models. Would you let someone who isn't a CPA file taxes for your business? Would you let a friend cut your hair just because they own scissors? IT is the same. It's a professional discipline. Treat it with the same seriousness you give to your legal, financial, and regulatory decisions.

And that last trope — the "tech-savvy cousin" one — is not an exception. If you aren't paying them to manage your IT or provide your business with tech support, then you are engaging in the care economy and failing to budget for critical expertise and infrastructure for your business.

The care economy is the idea of someone providing support or services to someone else without being paid financially for it. It's often used when describing how children will help with caretaking responsibilities for elderly parents, but it has relevance in business context when business owners will have a friend or family member fill a critical business role without being paid for it (like a wife handling the bookkeeping for a business or someone's brother helping every once in a while with a website issue or with setting up new email addresses for the business). **Do this long enough, and your business. Will. Fail.**

The Signs It's Time to Outsource IT

You probably need help if:

- You're managing two or more users and devices. (The more you manage, the more obvious the sign that it's time.)
- You've started hiring remote workers or contractors.
- You're holding sensitive client data (think legal, financial, and healthcare).

- You've had one too many close calls with ransomware or outages.

- You want to improve security but don't know where to start.

- You're spending more than an hour a week fiddling with settings, updates, or access.

- You're noticing that each person operates in a silo completely independently of everyone else, either in their workflow, tech stack, or both.

It's not just about tech issues — it's about time, risk, and scale. If your business has become reliant on technology (which is very nearly EVERY BUSINESS EVER), you need someone who specializes in protecting and optimizing it.

Why IT Matters at Any Size

Even if you're only using a few tools (Google Workspace, Box, and a CRM), you benefit from:

- Better response time when something fails

- Proactive patches and protections

- Guidance on avoiding blind spots and wasted spending

Refer back to Chapter 6. "Security That Scales" Nearly every security measure discussed in that chapter assumes you have some level of proactive or strategic IT support in place. Without it, even the best tools can be misconfigured or underutilized.

The best IT support scales with you. Start lean but start smart.

Questions to Ask an IT Partner Before You Sign Anything

- Do you *specialize* in businesses of our size and industry? The smaller your business, the more critical this question is.

CHAPTER 12. WHEN (AND HOW) TO
OUTSOURCE IT THE SMART WAY

- How many other clients do you **currently** have who are our size? This question helps to confirm that they are actually used to supporting your company size, not just "open to it."
- What does onboarding look like. How long? How disruptive?
- Do you help with vendor management (dealing with internet providers, SaaS tool vendors)?
- How do you handle support tickets? What's your response time?
- In what kinds of situations would we need to pay for billable time outside of the normal recurring billing arrangement? This answer can range widely from company to company, so it is critical in helping you compare different companies without getting any nasty surprises later.
- Can you help us budget for future tech needs?
- What tools or platforms do you support? What tools or platforms don't you support?
- How do you help us stay compliant (HIPAA, FINRA)?

Watch how they answer. If you get vague replies, sales buzzwords, or lots of "we'll figure that out later," walk away.

Red Flags to Watch Out For

- They try to push you into new hardware or equipment without clear arguments for why.
- They won't give you admin access "for your protection."
- They don't document anything or share reports with you.
- They avoid clear pricing or nickel-and-dime you on every ticket.
- They don't talk about security or backups until *you* bring it up.

If it feels like they're building dependence instead of empowerment, **that's not a partner — it's a liability**. Delegation to an IT provider helps you focus. But if they have too many hidden fees and don't even help you with strategic planning or budgeting, walk away.

Don't Abdicate — Delegate

Outsourcing doesn't mean checking out. Ultimate liability and responsibility still rest with you. You're still the business owner.

You still need to:

♦ Review reports.

♦ Ask questions.

♦ Hold them accountable.

♦ Know the basics of how your systems work.

The goal isn't to become an IT expert. It's to become an **informed leader** who delegates wisely. Failing to stay involved can lead to problems and not necessarily small ones. If you don't keep your vendors honest—and they are supposed to monitor critical infrastructure but don't — it's not just about paying a vendor not to do their job.

I've seen entire businesses fail when they've gotten hit by a ransom attack. And they only found out then that their vendors failed to ensure the proper tools for recovery and prevention weren't working. You can play the blame game if you want. You wouldn't be wrong to say your IT company failed you. But does it really matter when you still have to close down your business because of it?

Audit Your IT Provider: Trust. But Verify

Once you've chosen an IT provider — whether it's a solo consultant, an MSP, or a comanaged arrangement — the next challenge is making sure they're actually doing what they promised. And not just technically … strategically too.

Think of this as an annual checkup. You don't want to wait until something breaks, gets hacked, or is irretrievable before you evaluate whether your IT provider is effective.

Ask for an Annual IT Review

- Treat your provider like a partner, not a vendor. Trust their intent and mission but keep them accountable.
- Ask them to provide a **written report** or presentation once a year that covers:
    - The current state of your infrastructure.
    - Security vulnerabilities and what's been patched.
    - Licensing and renewal dates.
    - Backup status reports.
    - Support ticket trends (what's causing repeated issues?).
    - Any recommended upgrades or strategic shifts.

If they act like this is an unreasonable request, that's a red flag. Transparency is basic stuff. If they can't — or won't — be open with you here, that's a big problem.

Schedule an Independent Security Audit

- Every one to two years, bring in a **third-party security firm** to audit your IT environment.

- You're not trying to catch your IT team in a lie. You're trying to catch what they may have missed. Being able to recognize and note this distinction can make the difference between a toxic vendor and a trusted partner in your business.

- This creates a layered safety net and fosters accountability and proactiveness. Your relationship with your IT team improves, and they'll also sleep better knowing they're protecting you even better than before.

Bonus: Many insurance providers (especially for cyber liability coverage) view independent audits as risk-reducing and may lower your premiums. Check with your insurance carrier or broker to see if they offer something similar; if not, it might be time to shop around (see "How to Shop for a Policy without Getting Screwed" in Chapter 4. "Cyber Liability Insurance: Your Financial Firewall" for more on this).

Know What to Look For

When reviewing your IT provider's performance, ask yourself:

- Are they proactive or only reactive?
- Do they help with budgeting and forecasting?
- Are you confident they could respond to a breach or disaster?
- Do they explain things in plain English?
- Have your IT needs outgrown their capabilities?

Note that there can be many reasons why this hasn't happened yet. So, if the answer to any of these questions is "no," it's worth a proper conversation with them. If they can't or won't address these concerns, then it might be time to revisit your support model.

You don't need to be a tech expert to spot red flags. You just need to ask the right questions and hold your IT provider to the same standard you'd expect from your accountant, lawyer, or payroll company.

Why "Too Small" Is a Myth

One of the biggest misconceptions I run into *by far* is a small business owner who thinks they're too small to need IT support ("I'm just a solo consultant" or "We only have four people. We don't need all that yet.).

Here's the reality: Every modern business, regardless of size, is powered by technology. And when tech breaks — or worse, when it's breached — it doesn't matter if you have one staff member or 100. The damage is real either way.

If anything, **small businesses are more vulnerable** because they don't have in-house resources or backup plans. A one-person firm can't afford to be down for three days troubleshooting email delivery or recovering from a ransomware incident.

You don't need to wait until you're a "real company" to benefit from outsourcing. Successful deployment of managed services has been shown to reduce IT costs by 25–45% and boost operational efficiency by as much as 65%.[23] That's leverage you can't afford to ignore *especially* when you're still small.

The sooner, the better.

Real-World Example: Small Team, Big Rescue

I once helped a two-person legal firm that had all their documents stored locally on a single laptop. That laptop crashed the night before a major filing deadline. They had no backups, no IT vendor, no clue what went wrong — just a lot of panic.

We were able to recover the data in time (barely), but it was a close call. They signed on for managed IT services the next week. Now their files are backed up, their email is secure, and they've never missed a deadline since.

Here's the truth:

- ◆ You don't need 20 employees to justify getting help.

- ◆ You don't need to wait until something breaks to start caring.

- ◆ You don't need a dedicated, in-house IT department.

- ◆ You just need someone who's thinking about this, *so you don't have to.*

If you're running payroll, client services, or project delivery on a laptop or in the cloud, you already depend on IT. So, it's not a matter of *if* you need support — it's a question of *how* you're going to get it before something costly goes wrong.

Getting help isn't overkill — it's responsible leadership.

Case Stories: Smart IT Outsourcing in Action

These stories show how outsourcing IT can either save a business from spinning its wheels or supercharge its growth with the right partner.

Nonprofit: Cheap Help, Expensive Lessons

Background: A nonprofit with a staff of 12 worked with a solo IT contractor who billed hourly and responded only when called. There was no proactive monitoring, no backup system, and no real documentation.

The Problem: After a routine Windows update broke several staff logins, no one could access their files for two days. The contractor was busy with another client and didn't respond for 48 hours.

The Fix: The organization moved to a managed IT services provider. They implemented monitoring, a password manager, automated backups, and transitioned to cloud-based document storage with shared permissions.

The Outcome: Since switching, downtime has dropped to nearly zero. Staff report faster support and better collaboration, and leadership no longer worries about being "tech paralyzed."

Lesson Learned: Pay now or pay later. Proactive support prevents painful breakdowns and loss of productivity.

Engineering Firm: From Reactive to Strategic

Background: A 14-person structural engineering firm initially had internal IT handled by their office manager. It worked when they were five people. But, as they grew, tech issues consumed more time and nothing scaled.

The Problem: New software rollouts took weeks. Devices weren't standardized. Security gaps were mounting. And no one owned the roadmap.

The Fix: They hired an MSP who performed a tech audit, aligned systems, implemented role-based security, and began quarterly vCIO meetings.

The Outcome: In one year, the company gained stronger infrastructure, consistent onboarding/offboarding, better remote access, and a clear long-term plan. They also reduced tech waste by consolidating tools.

Lesson Learned: Real growth needs real IT strategy. Smart out-sourcing is less about fixing problems and more about removing them before they start.

The TL;DR

♦ If you're spending time troubleshooting tech issues, putting out fires, or wondering how secure your systems are, it's probably time to outsource.

♦ Break/Fix is reactive. MSPs are proactive. Fractional strategists (like vCIOs) help you plan for scale. Know which type you need.

♦ The best combo for small, professional service firms is an MSP with strategic support layered on top.

♦ Even if you're small, you still need real IT support. Scalable solutions aren't just for big companies.

♦ Ask pointed questions. Look for transparency, industry familiarity, and a proactive approach.

♦ Watch for red flags (vague pricing, lack of documentation, hidden fees, unclear responsibilities).

♦ Delegating doesn't mean disappearing. You're still accountable, so stay involved.

♦ A failed IT provider can tank your business. Vet them like your company's future depends on it — because it does.

Once you've got IT support in place, it's time to think about growth.

Whether you're hiring your first assistant or building out a team, the next chapter offers a clear roadmap for growing your business without letting your tech fall behind.

CHAPTER 13

The IT Growth Plan: From 1 to 20 and Beyond

Growth Needs to Be Intentional

Let's face it: Most small businesses don't plan their IT for growth. They just react to it.

You hire someone, and suddenly you're scrambling to buy a new laptop. You add a contractor, and now you're duplicating Google Docs and forwarding emails manually. Before you know it, your "system" is duct tape, favors, and a spreadsheet with half the passwords missing. (Also, PLEASE get a password manager!)

This chapter is about getting *ahead* of your IT needs, not behind them. Whether you're solo, managing a handful of people, or scaling to 20 and beyond, you need a plan that grows with you, **not one that collapses under its own weight**.

Stage 1. Solo Doesn't Mean Sloppy

Even if it's just you, you still need a solid IT foundation:

- ◆ Use a business-grade productivity suite (Google Workspace or Microsoft 365).
- ◆ Set up a password manager from Day 1. (*Trust* me on this.)
- ◆ Use MFA everywhere, even on your phone and your laptop.
- ◆ Choose tools with centralized administration and role-based permissions.

This is the stuff that makes you look professional *and* makes your life easier. You're not "too small" for proper IT. You're building habits now that will pay off tenfold later.

And here's the kicker: If you *don't* build this foundation, it's going to bite you later. The moment you decide to bring someone else into your business — whether that's a contractor, a virtual assistant, or a full-time hire — you'll realize how painful it is to transition from "everything lives in my head" to "how do I onboard someone cleanly and securely?" Your personal Gmail suddenly feels like a terrible idea. Even if you're not sure you'll ever hire someone, it's still so much better to be safe than sorry.

Stage 2. The First Hires: Structure Before You Scale

When you bring on your first team member — whether a contractor or a full-time employee — you need to shift from "my stuff" to **"our system."** More than half of small businesses (51%) struggle to streamline systems as they grow.[24] Without intentional IT structure, every new hire compounds the chaos.

That means:

- Shared Drives or SharePoint Sites (no more emailing files back and forth, no more stashing things just on your computer or in your personal OneDrive or Dropbox)
- Company-owned accounts (not "just use your Gmail")
- Clear onboarding checklists and offboarding procedures
- Defined roles with structured permissions (see "Shared Drives and Shared Sites Done Right" in Chapter 7. "User Access and Risk Management")

You're setting up the rails now so you don't crash the train later.

Contractor or Employee? Full-Time or Part-Time? IT Implications You Can't Ignore

When you're growing beyond a solo setup, one of the first decisions you'll face is whether to bring someone on as a **1099 contractor** or a **W-2 employee**, closely followed by whether you want to hire them part time or full time. Most people think about this strictly in terms of HR, payroll, or taxes. Sure, those matter. But this choice also has **major IT implications** that are often overlooked.

Let's break it down.

Control vs. Convenience

W-2 employees give you more control, plain and simple. You can:

- Define exactly when and how they work on your business, especially during business hours.
- Set them up with internal access to your company's systems (email, storage, calendar, task management).
- Issue company-owned devices with security and monitoring in place.

- ♦ Enforce your cybersecurity, backup, and access policies without needing special contractual workarounds.

Contractors? Not so much.

You should aim to **keep contractors outside of your internal systems whenever possible**. Only share the specific data and tools they need to complete their narrowly scoped work. Don't give blanket access to email accounts, company-wide file drives, or admin-level tools.

The most egregious — and common — example of this happening is hiring a VA or EA but engaging with them as a 1099 contractor rather than hiring them outright as a W-2 employee.

With 1099s, you're often working with **personal devices and personal software**, and you can't require them to change their behavior unless it's explicitly in your contract. Even then, you're limited by labor laws and practical enforcement challenges.

And, if you care about client confidentiality, HIPAA/FINRA compliance, or business continuity, that lack of control becomes a real liability fast.

You Can't Secure What You Don't Control

Imagine this: You hire a contractor, give them access to client files, and months later they leave. Do they still have access? Are those files still sitting on their personal laptop? Did they share them with anyone else? You may never know.

That's the danger of defaulting to BYOD and contractor setups without clear boundaries.

This doesn't mean you can't hire contractors. But it does mean you need to think twice about what kind of access they need, and whether that level of access makes more sense with a W-2 structure.

Another way of looking at this: If you have a contractor who has a business computer and full internal access, nine times out of 10 you're probably better off hiring them officially as a W-2 employee.

The Hybrid Approach

One smart middle ground is to **issue a company-managed device** to contractors who need access to sensitive systems. You still get control over security settings but maintain the flexibility of a 1099 relationship. If that's not practical, then **limit their access** to only the tools and data absolutely required and always use business accounts — not personal ones.

Also: Whatever you decide, **document it**. Include IT expectations in your contractor agreements (MFA, secure storage, and whether you reserve the right to audit or remove access).

Budget Impacts (and Hidden Costs)

Sure, a 1099 might seem cheaper up front: no benefits, no payroll tax, no equipment to issue. But factor in the **long-term IT tradeoffs**:

- Less control over how your data is accessed
- Higher risk of misconfiguration or data leakage
- Increased support complexity for mixed environments

By contrast, W-2 staff may cost more on paper, but you gain **standardization, compliance, and IT simplicity**, which pays dividends as you grow.

Part-Time vs. Full-Time: Hidden IT Costs You Didn't Budget For

Here's a mistake I see a lot of small business owners make: They hire **multiple part-time people** when they could've — *and should've* — hired a **single full-time person**.

Why? Usually, it's to avoid paying benefits. On paper, three part-timers working 10–15 hours a week each seem equivalent to one full-timer. Same total hours, less overhead.

But your IT costs aren't scaled by hours worked. They're scaled by headcount.

Every part-time person still needs:

♦ A licensed business email account

♦ A spot in your password manager

♦ Access to shared drives or systems

♦ A properly configured laptop or desktop (ideally business-issued)

That means three part-timers will cost nearly **three times more from an IT perspective** than one full-time hire. You're tripling your software licenses, device management needs, support tickets, and onboarding/offboarding burden.

Unless there's a very good reason (like highly specialized skills), you're almost always better off consolidating those roles into **one full-time employee with standardized access and setup**. Your IT provider will thank you. Your budget will too.

👍 **RULE OF THUMB**

If the person is ...

- ♦ handling sensitive client data
- ♦ accessing core systems regularly
- ♦ part of the long-term vision

... then strongly consider a **W-2 employee** with a company-issued device.

If they're ...

- ♦ handling a specific, short-term deliverable
- ♦ not accessing internal systems or client records
- ♦ doing low-risk, external work

... then a **contractor setup** might be just fine — as long as you don't cut corners on access controls. ●

Feeling overwhelmed? I know how it feels. I've helped hundreds of solopreneurs scale to include their first true staff. Even if you're not prepared for *managed* IT services, don't be shy about leveraging IT consultatively at this stage — preferably before you make a costly mistake.

Stage 3. 5–10 People: Time to Get Proactive

Once your team starts growing, you *can't* be the IT person anymore. Period. When tech is duct-taped together, growth starts to really hurt. In fact, 43% of small businesses say a lack of technical know-how is actively holding them back.[25] You can't scale on hope alone. You need systems that grow with you and the expertise to facilitate them.

You should have:

- A managed IT provider or internal resource (even part-time) for day-to-day support
- A basic tech policy (what's okay to use, what's not)
- Regular security training and phishing awareness
- Tools with centralized admin control (no rogue Dropbox or personal Gmail accounts, please)
- Regularly tested backups and continuity plans

You're in growth mode now. Act like it. Your systems need to be reliable, recoverable, and reportable.

Stage 4. 10–20+ People: IT as a Strategic Lever

At this stage, IT stops being "just infrastructure" and becomes a **business enabler**. It's no longer about keeping the lights on — it's about making decisions that improve efficiency, margins, and client experience. A 10% impact to your business' productivity starts to take on a different flavor in this range. The dollars really start to pile up now.

You need:

- Strategic planning (ideally with a vCIO or fractional IT leader)
- Annual IT budgets and roadmap sessions
- Auditable policies and compliance frameworks
- Advanced integrations between systems (CRM, billing, task management)
- Performance monitoring and capacity planning

This is when businesses that invested early start to **leap ahead**. And those that didn't? They stall or implode under the weight of technological mismanagement and "death by a thousand cuts."

Growth Without Burnout: Build Before You Break

You don't have to do everything at once. But you *do* have to keep pace with your business' growth.

The goal of this chapter — and really, this whole book — is to give you **the bones of a scalable IT plan** without burying you in jargon, costs, or decisions you don't need yet. So, here's your mantra:

Right-size today. Prebuild for tomorrow.

If you follow this rule, you'll be able to grow smoothly, stay secure, and maybe even get a little sleep at night.

Case Stories: IT That Grows with You

These stories follow small businesses as they grow from one person to many — and show how scalable IT foundations make all the difference.

Solo Business Coach: Hired Help, No Headaches

Background: A solo business coach used a personal Gmail account, Dropbox, and stored client notes in Google Docs. She never intended to grow a team but ended up needing an assistant and a part-time content marketer.

The Problem: Sharing passwords and files quickly became a mess. She worried about confidentiality, lost a contract draft in an overwritten file, and realized she had no offboarding plan.

The Fix: Her IT consultant helped her migrate to Google Workspace, implement LastPass for Business, and use Shared Drives for client documents with clear access control.

The Outcome: Hiring became plug-and-play. Her assistant could manage tasks without compromising client privacy, and turnover became a five-minute checklist.

Lesson Learned: Even if you *think* you'll stay solo, don't build like it. Good systems don't punish growth — they enable it.

Engineering Team: From Startup to Serious

Background: A two-person engineering startup landed their first big municipal project and knew they needed to grow. They'd been using personal devices and file storage up to that point.

The Problem: They brought on four new hires but had no onboarding workflow, no centralized accounts, and no access management. One new hire accidentally shared sensitive drawings with the wrong contact.

The Fix: They partnered with an IT provider who established an onboarding/offboarding process, implemented Microsoft 365 with SharePoint, enabled MFA, and added IRONSCALES and Spanning.

The Outcome: Within three months, their internal ops ran like a much larger company. Clients noticed the professionalism. Bidding on bigger projects became easier thanks to new compliance protocols.

Lesson Learned: You don't wait to scale *and then* get organized — you get organized *so you can* scale.

The TL;DR

- Plan for growth even if you think you'll stay small. Solo doesn't mean sloppy.
- Build your IT foundation early (password manager, MFA, centralized file storage).

- First hires should get company accounts, shared drives, and onboarding/offboarding processes.

- Don't default to 1099 contractors if you need internal access or control. Consider W-2 status instead.

- Contractors should be kept outside core systems unless absolutely necessary.

- One full-time employee is almost always more IT-efficient than multiple part-timers. IT costs scale by headcount, not hours.

- Document and enforce IT expectations in every role, including part-time and contract work.

- With more than a staff of five, invest in proactive, managed IT services and support (internal or external).

- With more than a staff of 10, use IT strategically. Let strategic vCIO power your growth.

Growth looks different when your team isn't all in the same room. Remote work brings flexibility, but it also requires better systems.

In the next chapter, we'll explore what it takes to build a secure, smooth-running remote team from an IT perspective.

CHAPTER 14

Remote Work Done Right: IT for Distributed Teams

Most Small Businesses Are Remote Now

One of the best silver linings to come out of COVID-19 was the fundamental shift we made toward embracing remote work. Remote work isn't going anywhere — and that's a good thing! It opens doors to talent, flexibility, and scalability. But it also opens floodgates for bad habits if you don't build the right IT foundation from the start.

Why Remote Teams Need a Different IT Discipline

In a physical office, you can sometimes get away with sloppy practices (shared logins, USB file transfers, and Post-it notes with passwords). I'm not saying these are appropriate, but a physical office is more forgiving of these practices. In a distributed team, those shortcuts become dangerous.

Without a plan, you get:

- Devices with no encryption or antivirus software
- Employees using personal email or storage
- No way to revoke access to company data if someone leaves
- No central record of who has what tools or data

You can't fix what you can't see. Remote IT must be intentional. And flexible work isn't a trend — it's an expectation. When given the option, 87% of people choose to work flexibly.[26] If your systems don't support that reality, you're not just behind —you're losing talent.

Essential Remote Infrastructure

The must-haves below have already been covered in detail earlier in the book, but they become even more critical for remote teams where IT sprawl and access control can spiral quickly. Here's a reminder of what's nonnegotiable:

Cloud-First Productivity Stack

- Google Workspace or Microsoft 365 (with centralized control)
- Shared Drives or SharePoint Sites (not personal storage or shared Dropbox folders)

Business-Grade Password Management

- LastPass Business, Dashlane for Business, or 1Password Teams
- Central admin control and offboarding tools

Remote-Capable Endpoint Protection

- EDR tools (SentinelOne, CrowdStrike) with cloud-management console
- Works no matter where the laptop is

SaaS Backup (like Spanning)

- ◆ Covers cloud email, files, calendars, contacts
- ◆ Automated and admin-accessible

In addition to the core stack, here are a few more essentials specific to distributed teams to ensure privacy, security, and productivity:

MDM

- ◆ Must be able to remotely wipe devices if lost or stolen
- ◆ Lightweight MDMs (Addigy or Intune) that are great for small teams

Team Communication Platform

- • Slack or Microsoft Teams
- • Promotes real-time, secure communication across locations

VPN Software

- ◆ For securing connections on public or home Wi-Fi
- ◆ Adds an extra layer of protection, especially for accessing sensitive data

Device Management Basics (Even for Small Teams)

You don't need a full-blown, enterprise-level MDM platform to get started. But yes, even small businesses should *absolutely* use MDM. It's one of the easiest and most impactful ways to protect your business when devices are out of reach.

Here's what you need to enforce:

- ◆ **MDM:** Lightweight options (Addigy, Mosyle, Intune) allow you to push updates, revoke access, and remotely wipe lost or stolen devices.

- **Full-disk encryption:** Use FileVault (Mac) or BitLocker (Windows). This isn't optional. If your business is regulated under HIPAA, FINRA, or other data-protection laws, this is a *legal requirement*. And it's important to note that only the Pro version of Windows has BitLocker; if you're using Home versions, it's time to upgrade.

- **Business-managed devices:** Always prefer devices enrolled under your business, not personal machines. It's the only way to ensure full control of your digital assets. This doesn't mean you can't have a BYOD policy in place. But you start off immediately making compromises to your policies when you can't enforce which software stays installed on personal computers or whether they have hard-drive encryption.

Remote doesn't mean less secure — it just requires stronger planning.

Remote Onboarding and Offboarding Checklist

Remote teams rely on a strong first impression. When onboarding is smooth, it builds confidence right away. When offboarding is sloppy, it leaves your company wide open to risk.

Onboarding is already tricky, but it's even harder when you're remote. In fact, 36% of remote employees found their onboarding experience confusing, slightly higher than their in-office counter-parts.[27] Clear processes make all the difference here.

Whether you're adding your first assistant or growing into a 15-person remote team, these checklists help you handle both scenarios securely and consistently. Feel free to use the following checklists and expand them to suit your exact needs.

Onboarding

- Provision laptop with required apps.

- Add to Google Workspace / Microsoft 365, Shared Drives, Slack/Teams.
- Issue password-manager credentials and guide.
- Schedule brief security orientation.

Offboarding

- Disable all cloud accounts.
- Lock password manager access.
- Wipe or reclaim laptop.
- Change shared credentials if applicable.

Build Your Remote Culture around Security

Remote doesn't mean disconnected. But you have to build habits:

- Encourage Slack/Teams messages like, "Does this email look sketchy?"
- Make use of channels in Slack/Teams to build team dynamics rather than 1:1 direct messages.
- Have verbal verification rules for money movement or file requests.
- Celebrate reported phishing attempts as wins — and don't forget to celebrate wins in general!

Lesson Learned

Remote work doesn't increase IT risk — it reveals it. If your systems only work inside your building, they were never secure in the first place.

But here's the upside: Distributed teams that commit to the right IT setup tend to become *more* secure, not less. They lean into structure, adopt better habits, and think critically about how data moves across their business. Remote work isn't just a challenge to overcome. It's an opportunity to modernize, simplify, and secure your systems in ways that help your business scale.

The right IT setup also saves money. Remote teams don't require physical office space, which means you're not on the hook for rent, utilities, or office upkeep. That's budget you can reallocate toward better tools, better security, and better talent.

The TL;DR

- Remote work isn't inherently risky. It just exposes weak IT practices that were already present.

- A solid remote IT foundation includes a cloud-based productivity suite, business-grade password management, endpoint protection, backups, MDM, VPNs, and a team-communication tool.

- Full-disk encryption and managed devices aren't optional for regulated industries — they're required.

- Onboarding and offboarding must be intentional, repeatable, and secure.

- Security culture matters. Encourage transparency, verification, and small daily wins.

- Remote work reduces office overhead and enables smarter investments in your tech stack.

Remote work has changed the way IT and HR interact. That connection matters most during onboarding, monitoring, and offboarding.

In the next chapter, we'll explore how hiring and security overlap, and how to protect your business from the inside.

PART V

Lessons from the Trenches

CHAPTER 15

Where HR Meets IT: Security, Monitoring, and Onboarding

Why HR and IT Are More Intertwined Than Ever

Roughly half of small businesses keep HR in-house, often to save money. But here's the problem: More than 80% of those decision-makers lack formal HR training, education, or even confidence in their own abilities.[28] When you combine that with IT access decisions, it's a recipe for overlooked risks.

So, it's a 50-50 split whether you are the HR department or you've outsourced that role to a fractional HR provider. Leaving aside the question of whether or not you should (*you should!*), the principles in this chapter still apply: If you've outsourced, share this chapter with your HR vendor; if you're solo or otherwise still handle the HR in-house, consider these best practices for yourself:

♦ Digital trust starts at hiring.

♦ Security policies are no longer just "IT issues." They begin with the hiring process.

♦ HR is your first line of defense against insider threats, fraud, and compliance failures.

Background Checks and Prehire Risk Screening

For many small businesses, background checks might feel like overkill. But, when it comes to protecting your data, your clients, and your reputation, **the hiring process is your first security gateway**. HR typically owns this step, but that doesn't mean IT should stay silent.

Some tools are more security-conscious than others, and many modern, background-check platforms can integrate directly into your HR dashboards, identity-management tools, or onboarding checklists. That means you can reduce manual handoffs, log actions for compliance, and ensure clean, consistent documentation.

Here's where screening can be useful:

♦ **Background checks** for criminal history or prior fraud

♦ **Fingerprinting**, especially for financial or other high-compliance roles

♦ **Employment verification** to avoid falsified experience

♦ **Social media checks** to surface public behavior that may be at odds with your company's values or industry requirements

♦ **Credit checks** when relevant to financial access or fiduciary duty

♦ **Drug and alcohol screening**, depending on the nature of the role and regional laws

From an IT perspective, here are some important considerations:

♦ **Choose tools** that integrate cleanly with your existing systems.

- Enable automated workflows to reduce risk of skipped steps or human error.
- Ensure there's an audit trail for accountability and legal protection.

Your HR provider or internal HR lead (*you!*) should always make the final call on what's appropriate, legal, and ethical. But don't overlook the opportunity for IT to streamline, secure, and support these processes from the ground up.

Onboarding: The First Security Policy Your Employee Signs

Onboarding isn't just an HR process. It's also your first opportunity to set expectations for security, device use, and access policies. This is where IT and HR must collaborate closely.

IT can help identify and advise HR on which onboarding policies are best practices from security and infrastructure standpoints. HR then makes the final determination on how to implement these policies in a way that aligns with employment law, regulatory compliance, and company culture.

Your onboarding process should include:

- Acceptable use policy (addressing the (mis)use of company equipment and software for personal reasons)
- Company-owned vs. personal devices
- Access control and data usage policies
- Language to obtain legal consent for/acknowledgement of IT monitoring and device auditing
- IP ownership clauses (work created on business time = company property)

♦ Using templates in your HR platform or digital signature tools to enforce consistency

Your onboarding document package should be standardized and easy to deploy, ideally with:

♦ A new user account setup form that includes which systems they'll need access to

♦ An IT security and acceptable-use policy

♦ A signed acknowledgment that company property, whether data or devices, remains with the company

♦ Any necessary opt-in for device monitoring (if applicable in your jurisdiction — HR should know!)

Also, consider scheduling a 30-minute IT onboarding walkthrough with each new hire. This provides a hands-on tour of tools, communication expectations, and instruction on how to avoid common security missteps. Whether or not that means delegating to a managed IT provider or doing it yourself, this walkthrough will prevent many potential struggles for new hires to adopt your tech stack.

Monitoring: What's Legal, What's Practical, What's Ethical

Monitoring can feel like a loaded word, especially for small businesses that pride themselves on a culture of trust. But done right — and with transparency — it's not about micromanagement. It's about protecting the business and the people in it.

As a business owner, you have a right (and a responsibility) to know how company resources are being used, where your data is going, and whether systems are secure. (This impacts many areas of your business, from internal administrative efficiency to the cost of insurance premiums. Say it again with me: **It's not about trust!**) But that right varies based on **what you own**, **who the worker is**, and **where they are located**.

Here's how to think about monitoring through a modern, risk-based lens:

- ◆ EDR tools (SentinelOne, CrowdStrike)
- ◆ Device monitoring (Addigy, Intune, DattoRMM)
- ◆ Geofencing/remote wipe tools (Prey GPS, Find My Mac)
- ◆ Productivity and activity tracking (Toggl, Hubstaff)
- ◆ Monitoring for:
  - ◆ **Remote vs. in-office staff:** There's little operational difference here for small businesses. The main difference in monitoring that comes to mind is local network monitoring in the office, which isn't noticeable to your staff. What matters most here is clarity. Whether someone is down the hall or across the country, make sure they know what's being monitored and why, and how that aligns with your company policies.
  - ◆ **BYOD vs. company-issued devices:** Ownership drives permission. You can freely monitor company-owned devices. But, if someone is using a personal device — even to access work files—you'll need explicit consent (and maybe legal review) to set up any monitoring or protection. (See "BYOD vs. Company-Owned: Choose Your Adventure (Wisely)" "Your Machines Age: Know How to Budget and When to Upgrade" and "You Can't Secure What You Don't Control" in Chapter 13. "The IT Growth Plan: From 1 to 20 and Beyond.")

Before you install monitoring software, ask yourself:

- ◆ Do I *own* the device?

- ◆ Have I disclosed my monitoring policy in onboarding?
- ◆ Is this level of monitoring necessary for the role?

Transparency is key. The goal is to detect and reduce risk, not spy on people. You're monitoring *systems*, not people (see "A Note on Screen Recording and Keyloggers" in this chapter). This is why most of the monitoring tools in the above list focus on protecting from security threats and protecting company data from falling into the wrong hands.

When done ethically and proportionally, monitoring *builds* trust. It shows you're serious about protecting company data without creeping into personal territory.

A Note on Screen Recording and Keyloggers

While technically available, screen-recording tools and keyloggers are rarely worth the risk or the damage to morale. From a practical standpoint, they almost never catch anything actionable or useful. From a psychological standpoint, they can completely erode trust.

Even if you frame it as a productivity tool, it's going to be received as a surveillance tactic. These tools are fundamentally based on a lack of trust. When your staff senses that, they disengage. Morale drops. Turnover increases. And risks of both negligent and malicious cyber incidents increase dramatically as a result.

Instead, focus on things like endpoint security, time-tracking tools, and access logs. These give you plenty of insight without making your team feel like they're being watched.

Termination Protocols

Most small businesses have a plan for bringing someone on, but few have a detailed plan for how to exit them. Whether it's a planned departure or a sudden, messy one, **offboarding is just as important as onboarding**. If you skip it or rush it, you expose your systems to security, legal, and reputational risks.

That said, there are some differences between voluntary vs. involuntary terminations:

♦ **Voluntary exits:** In the cases of resignation, retirement, or a new job, you usually have some notice. Preschedule account deactivation, confirm file handoffs, and do a final device check. These are preferred when possible because it gives everyone more time to digest and prepare. The reduced stress also helps reduce errors during this process.

♦ **Involuntary exits:** Layoffs and terminations for cause should be handled swiftly and securely. Ideally, IT should be notified *before* the conversation, so they can prepare to revoke access in real time or with precise timing. (Seriously, *I cannot stress this enough*. Assuming IT is outsourced here, there will be details they know about access, deadlines, and obstacles that HR needs to be aware of in turn. Failing to give IT proper notice can seriously jeopardize an involuntary exit. Plan ahead as much as possible.)

♦ **Remote wipes:** Ensure all mobile or remote staff devices can be wiped if they're company-owned, or that access is restricted and company software and data are removed if they're BYOD.

♦ **Documentation:** Always include legal documentation confirming the return (or buyout) of company devices, data, and IP. This protects both parties.

- ◆ **Checklist:** Use your IT provider to help prepare a checklist in advance (see "Offboarding Is Where Most Breaches Begin" in Chapter 7. "User Access and Risk Management" and "Remote Onboarding and Offboarding Checklist" in Chapter 14. "Remote Work Done Right: IT for Distributed Teams").

Stressed again for emphasis: Don't leave the burden of offboarding to HR alone. IT should always, ALWAYS, **ALWAYS** be looped in as early as possible, so that access, devices, and licenses can be removed cleanly, predictably, and securely. Better yet, automate what you can. If your systems support it, use offboarding workflows in your HR systems to ensure nothing is missed.

Case Stories: Due Diligence in HR and When It Fails

Consulting Firm: Background Check Saves the Day

Background: A small consulting firm was hiring a VA to help with calendar management and light bookkeeping. The candidate aced the interview and came highly recommended.

The Problem: Just before the offer was finalized, the firm ran a background check. The report flagged prior convictions related to embezzlement and identity theft — charges that were not disclosed in the interview process.

The Fix: The hiring manager, with support from their fractional HR provider, rescinded the offer and documented the results for compliance.

The Outcome: The company avoided handing sensitive client and financial access to someone with a history of financial crimes.

Lesson Learned: Background checks are about common sense and due diligence. A simple screening step protects the business, its clients, and its reputation. Trust, but verify.

Marketing Agency: Offboarding Gone Wrong

Background: A marketing agency terminated a remote employee for poor performance. They assumed removing their email account was sufficient offboarding.

The Problem: The former employee still had active access to Slack, Google Drive, and Canva for two full weeks after termination. During that time, they deleted key project files, changed folder ownership, and posted negative messages in shared channels.

The Fix: The agency's IT provider was brought in urgently to secure access and restore deleted content. Legal counsel was consulted to begin damage control.

The Outcome: The business faced reputational harm with clients and internal disruption across several departments. Restoration efforts cost thousands.

Lesson Learned: Offboarding isn't just about email. Every account, platform, and permission must be reviewed, ideally with a checklist managed by IT.

Graphic Design Firm: Who Owns the IP?

Background: A graphic design firm allowed employees to use company-issued software on their work laptops, assuming staff would follow an informal "honor system" when it came to professional vs. personal work.

The Problem: After one designer resigned, they continued using the Adobe Creative Cloud license still active on their former company-issued laptop rather than purchasing their own. They used it to complete freelance projects for external clients. Months later, a legal dispute arose over the licensing of one of these designs, and the company was named in the lawsuit because the work had been created using software owned and licensed under the business.

The Fix: The firm worked with legal counsel to resolve the dispute and updated its acceptable use and IP policies to include language that clarified post-employment restrictions and software-use boundaries.

The Outcome: Although the company avoided heavy penalties, it incurred legal costs and reputational risk. They realized just how far responsibility can extend when software and devices aren't fully decommissioned.

Lesson Learned: IP issues aren't just about creative ownership. They're also about platform liability. Offboard thoroughly, shut down licenses, and clearly define postemployment use policies. Be crystal clear about IP ownership in onboarding, especially for creatives. Work done on your systems, on your time, or with your tools belongs to the business, so be careful about what that can mean for your business.

The TL;DR

- Hiring, onboarding, and offboarding are as much about IT as they are about HR. Plan both together.
- Use background checks and prehire screenings to reduce risk before granting access.
- Document device use, monitoring consent, and IP ownership during onboarding.

- Stick to ethical, transparent monitoring. Never spy, especially with screen recorders or keyloggers.
- BYOD requires special handling (written consent, restricted access, legal clarity).
- Always coordinate offboarding with IT. Don't let anyone leave with active logins.
- Build and automate HR/IT checklists to reduce risk and human error.

Even when your internal policies are dialed in, some industries face extra pressure.

If HIPAA, FINRA, or other compliance frameworks apply to you, the next chapter will help you meet the requirements without getting buried in complexity.

CHAPTER 16

Regulated But Resilient: IT for Compliance-Heavy Industries

Compliance-First Attitude

When you operate in a regulated industry, "good enough" IT just doesn't cut it. The stakes are higher, the rules are tighter, and the margin for error is slimmer.

HIPAA violations can cost anywhere from $100 to $50,000 per exposed patient record — and that's just the regulatory piece. For smaller practices, a data breach covered in local media can quickly spiral into lawsuits and long-term damage.[29] While I don't have statistics for other regulatory bodies like FINRA or SEC, it's safe to assume similar costs and fines could apply there.

Whether you're in finance, healthcare, or another compliance-heavy space, your IT systems don't just support your operations. They form the backbone of your regulatory posture.

The mindset shift is key: IT isn't just a set of tools. It's a **liability shield** when done right or a **compliance landmine** when done wrong.

For nonregulated businesses, decisions about platforms and practices are often driven by cost, ease of use, or team preferences. In a regulated space, **compliance becomes the filter** through which all tech decisions must pass:

♦ Can we retain records for the required duration?

♦ Is this vendor willing to sign a BAA?

♦ Does this platform offer the right kind of encryption?

You can still consider other factors like cost or ease of use, but you'll have fewer options.

In regulated industries, you're not just managing devices and apps. You're managing legal risk ... every single day.

Key Regulatory Frameworks Small Businesses Encounter

In the small business world, regulation often sneaks up on you. You don't need to be a hospital or a major investment firm to fall under federal rules. If you're a **small financial advisory firm**, a **healthcare clinic**, or a **medical billing contractor**, you're likely already subject to **FINRA**, **SEC**, or **HIPAA** — whether or not you've fully realized it.

Let's focus on two major frameworks that apply to the most common small-business sectors:

FINRA and SEC (Finance)

♦ If you deal with investments or securities, or act as a registered financial adviser, you're regulated by FINRA and possibly SEC.

♦ These agencies care deeply about:

  ♦ Retention of communications (email, chat, reports)

- WORM storage for audit trails and records
- Auditability of financial transactions
- Protection against unauthorized access
- You need IT systems that support long-term data retention (think six years or more, and aim for more than seven), secure access controls, and event logs that can't be tampered with.

HIPAA (Healthcare)

- If your business handles PHI — whether you're a provider, an administrator, or even a subcontractor — you're bound by HIPAA.
- HIPAA requirements include:
  - Encryption of PHI at rest *and* in transit
  - Controlled access with audit trails
  - Data-retention policies (minimum six or seven years, depending on state laws—aim for over seven)
  - Breach detection and response protocols
- What makes HIPAA particularly tricky is that **intent doesn't matter**. You could be violating HIPAA and not know it until something bad happens.

Documentation and Data Retention

Why logs, versioning, and backups matter more when you're regulated:

- In regulated industries, you're expected to be able to **reconstruct who did what, when, and how** — sometimes years after the fact.

- Audit trails aren't optional. They're your first line of legal defense in case of a complaint, an investigation, or a lawsuit.

- Versioning protects against accidental (or malicious) overwrites, especially when dealing with contracts, forms, or treatment plans.

- Backups must go beyond "restoring files." They need to prove continuity, security, and retention compliance.

- Good IT systems make this documentation automatic and tamper-proof, so you're not relying on human memory or email chains when it counts.

Other considerations:

- FINRA: Requires retention of certain communications (email, trade confirmations) for **at least six years**, and many documents must be immutable (WORM-compliant)

- HIPAA: Requires healthcare providers to retain medical records and audit logs for **a minimum of six to seven years** (depending your state) from the date of creation or the date they were last in effect

- Strategies for storing audit trails and maintaining version history:

  - Use platforms that offer immutable logging (WORM storage).

  - Schedule regular exports and backups with long-term retention options.

  - Store multiple copies in different geographic regions (if possible).

- Legal defensibility: "If it's not documented, it didn't happen."

- Regulators don't care how honest or well-intentioned your team is. They care whether you can produce logs, timestamps, and access records to prove it.

- Good documentation gives you more than a technical edge. It gives you a legal one.

- In a dispute, an audit, or a lawsuit, being able to show your work (and who accessed what, when) might be the difference between a small fix and a six-figure penalty.

IT Practices That Support Compliance

Compliance isn't just about policies and paperwork. It lives in the way your systems are configured and maintained every single day. The right practices reduce risk, improve audit readiness, and (importantly) make it easier to sleep at night.

Let's break down a few essentials:

Encryption at Rest and in Transit

- Your data must be protected **while it's stored** (on a server, hard drive, or cloud account) and **while it's moving** (via email, file transfer, or other data movement among internal systems).

- Encryption at rest helps prevent breaches if a device is stolen or lost.

- Encryption in transit guards against eavesdropping or interception during communication.

MFA and Identity-Access Control

- MFA ensures that even if a password is compromised, the account isn't.

♦ Identity-access control means giving people access **only to what they need**, not to everything. For example, an office assistant shouldn't have access to full patient records or investment portfolios.

Device and Endpoint Management

♦ Every laptop, phone, and desktop that touches your systems is a potential liability. **Beware of BYOD.**

♦ Device-management platforms (Intune, Addigy) allow you to enforce encryption, remote wipe lost devices, and verify software compliance.

♦ Think of this as your front line for hygiene and control.

Monitoring and Alerting for Suspicious Behavior

♦ You need systems that will flag unusual activity (login attempts from foreign countries, large file downloads, or after-hours access to sensitive data).

♦ Whether it's part of your antivirus software, a standalone SIEM, or part of a broader MSP/MSSP solution, you should have *eyes on the inside*.

Role-Based Permissions

♦ This one's simple: People should only have access to the data and tools required for their role.

♦ It's not just about security. It's about **minimizing the blast radius** if something goes wrong.

♦ It helps with audits. Regulators will want to know you've segmented access based on function and seniority.

Choose the Right Tools and Vendors

- Work only with vendors who can offer BAAs or equivalent for your industry.

- Use platform recommendations for regulated industries (Box. com over Google Drive, especially for HIPAA compliance).

- Be realistic. Strong cybersecurity standards like SOC 2 compliance is fantastic. But many small businesses won't be able to afford or find SOC 2-certified vendors tailored to sub-20 person companies. This is a good place to distinguish between:

  - **MSP** handles IT foundations (help desk, device support, backups).

  - **MSSP** focuses specifically — and sometimes explicitly/ exclusively — on security monitoring, detection, and compliance enforcement. (These are the companies that often bring SOC 2 compliance to the table, and they are often *much* more expensive than MSPs as well.)

  - Hiring either an MSP or MSSP does not *necessarily* negate the need for the other. There are times when you may need to engage in both, depending on their respective scopes of service.

What Auditors and Examiners Look For

Whether you're dealing with HIPAA, FINRA, or another regulatory body, the audit process isn't just about policies on paper. It's about what your IT systems can **prove**. Examiners are trained to spot gaps between what you say you're doing and what your logs, backups, and tools actually show.

Let's unpack what they look for — and how to prepare.

Common IT Red Flags in Compliance Audits

◆ **Lack of formal documentation:** There is no acceptable use policy, no security training logs, or no signed onboarding/offboarding procedures.

◆ **Inadequate backups:** These are systems that don't retain data long enough or lack immutability (WORM) features.

◆ **Shared user accounts:** If multiple people use one login, you can't track accountability.

◆ **No audit trails:** If you can't show who accessed what and when, you're out of luck.

◆ **Overpermissioned users:** Everyone with admin access or viewing rights to all records? That's a no-go.

◆ **No written disaster recovery or incident response plan:** If something goes wrong, regulators want to know you've planned for it.

Tips for Preparing for a FINRA, SEC, or HIPAA Review

◆ Conduct an **internal audit** or use a third party to do one annually.

◆ Keep your IT documentation organized, up to date, and in a central location.

◆ Test your backups — not just that they exist but that they work.

◆ Print out or export key logs and policies quarterly, just in case your software vendor has an outage during an audit.

◆ Have your IT provider participate in audit preparation. They should be able to help you defend your setup.

The Importance of Recurring Risk Assessments

- ◆ Compliance is never "set it and forget it." It's dynamic.
- ◆ At least once a year, assess:
  - ◆ Where your data lives
  - ◆ Who has access to it
  - ◆ Whether your tools and vendors still align with your compliance needs
- ◆ Document the process. Even if you don't make major changes, proving that you *evaluated* your risk posture can help immensely during an audit.

(See "Stay Current: Key Regulatory Resources" in Appendix C. "Resources.")

Case Stories: Regulatory Scares and Close Calls

Physical Therapy Practice: HIPAA Wake-Up Call

Background: A physical therapy practice used a local IT vendor to install their practice-management software on a front-desk employee's computer.

The Problem: The employee used this same device to access personal email, use social media, and run video calls. The machine contained unencrypted PII and PHI, violating HIPAA rules about how and where protected data can be stored.

The Fix: After a surprise audit triggered by a patient complaint, the clinic was cited and forced to engage a HIPAA compliance officer to oversee remediation.

The Outcome: They moved all PHI to a centralized, cloud-based platform, separated workstations by function, and changed IT vendors.

Lesson Learned: Never store PHI on a machine used for general internet access. HIPAA compliance isn't just about software. It's about how and where data lives.

Investment Firm: The FINRA Lockout

Background: A boutique investment firm relied on their Microsoft 365 account for email and file storage but had no formal email archiving or retention policies.

The Problem: During a routine FINRA exam, regulators requested archived correspondence and compliance records from several years back. The firm was unable to produce everything. Some records had been deleted or autopurged by default-retention rules.

The Fix: They implemented a third-party email archiving solution with higher than six-year, WORM-compliant retention, configured immutability rules, and engaged a consultant to revise their compliance posture.

The Outcome: The firm avoided fines but received a warning and had to submit to a secondary compliance review.

Lesson Learned: Regulated backups aren't optional. Understand your industry's rules and configure your tools accordingly.

The TL;DR

♦ Regulated businesses must build IT around compliance, not convenience.

- ◆ FINRA and HIPAA both require strict retention, encryption, and audit trails.

- ◆ Good documentation isn't optional. It's your legal safety net.

- ◆ Use tools with WORM storage, role-based access, and MFA.

- ◆ Vet vendors for BAAs (HIPAA) and archiving features (FINRA).

- ◆ Annual risk assessments help prevent surprises and show auditors you're serious.

- ◆ Your IT provider should help prepare for audits, not just fix problems after they happen.

Compliance matters. But so does resilience.

Before closing things out, I'll share real-world stories of small businesses that got it right, learned the hard way, or rebuilt after a scare. You'll see what success and failure actually look like in the wild.

CHAPTER 17

Bonus Case Studies: What It Looks Like in the Wild

Why IT Matters

Up until now, we've covered all the "what" and "how" of IT for small businesses. But this chapter is about the "why" — **why it matters** and what it actually looks like in a real businesses just like yours.

These aren't theoretical models. These are stories from the field — clients and contacts I've worked with over the years who've either nailed it, learned the hard way, or both.

What a Ransomware Attack Feels Like

Before we jump into the stories, I want to give you a visceral sense of what a ransomware attack actually feels like because no case study will hit as hard as **that moment** when it's *your* system and *your* data on the line.

Imagine opening your laptop one morning, only to find that none of your files open. Every document, every spreadsheet, every client folder has been renamed and encrypted. There's a flashing message on your screen demanding money — in Bitcoin, of course — with a countdown clock ticking ominously. It's not a prank. *It's real.*

Your gut drops. You scramble to see if you can undo it, maybe reboot. Nothing works. Your backup? Not working either — or worse, infected too. You try calling someone, *anyone*, to help. But your go-to tech person is unavailable or unable to help recover what isn't there. (No backups, remember.)

You can't work. You can't access client data. You're not sure what's been stolen or compromised. You feel helpless, exposed, and completely out of control. Your livelihood is frozen, possibly damaged beyond repair. And the worst part? You realize this might have been avoidable.

This chapter is filled with examples of businesses that either avoided that outcome or didn't. These are the cautionary tales and quiet wins that prove why IT strategy isn't optional anymore.

Case Stories: Successful Outcomes

Legal Firm: Dodging a Disaster

A small but growing law firm had just five employees when they called me in. They were using personal email accounts, saving files to local machines, and had *zero* backup plan. Not even Dropbox.

We implemented:

- Google Workspace with Shared Drives in Google Drive
- Spanning backup for emails and files

- IRONSCALES for phishing protection
- LastPass for Business to manage passwords

Three months later? They were hit with a phishing attack across all of their email accounts. Any one of them might have clicked on the message and compromised their email account. But IRONSCALES flagged the message and removed the suspicious message automatically across all of their inboxes. No downtime. No compromised accounts. No breached data. Just a quick fix and a big sigh of relief.

The managing partner later told me, "This was the first time I felt like our tech was working *for* us, not against us."

Financial Consultant Firm: DIY Nightmare

This solo financial consultant had been in business for 15 years. Great at client relationships, terrible at documentation and security. Everything was stored locally, client records lived in her inbox, and she relied on her nephew to "do the tech stuff." If you're familiar with the finance sector, you can already tell that she was violating FINRA and SEC regulations. You might think you know where I'm going with this ... but no. It gets worse.

Then she lost access to her email. Turns out, her domain had expired and was hijacked. She lost client trust overnight and spent thousands trying to untangle the mess.

We rebuilt her system using:

- Microsoft 365 for compliance and Outlook support
- Redtail CRM with proper governance and security for her client records
- Centralized, auditable file storage with Box
- A backup solution for Microsoft 365 emails

- A referral for — and assistance with — obtaining cyber liability insurance

She's still in business but barely survived. We weren't able to get the original domain back because it had expired, and a client's trust, once broken, is difficult to repair. She was luckier than most. She was able to bounce back.

Lesson learned the hard way: **DIY stops being cute when you're storing other people's financial data**.

Coaching Team: Scaling Smoothly

This three-person coaching team knew they wanted to grow, but they didn't want to lose their lean and flexible model. They were already using Google Workspace but needed help formalizing things.

We helped them:

- Create a shared folder structure and standardize naming (Shared Drives with role-based permissions, no "spiderweb" of sharing individual files and folders with each other).
- Set up onboarding templates for new coaches.
- Implement MFA and a centralized password manager.
- Automate client intake using Google Forms + Zapier.

By the time they hit 10 people, onboarding a new coach took less than 30 minutes, and clients never noticed the difference in delivery. That's what scaling looks like when your backend is clean.

The TL;DR

- A ransomware attack is terrifying, paralyzing, and usually avoidable.

◆ Good IT is invisible until you need it — and then it's everything.

◆ Even the smallest businesses need a professional IT foundation. Size is not an excuse.

◆ DIY IT can lead to financial loss, reputational damage, and regulatory violations, especially in the legal and financial sectors.

◆ A clean, centralized, and standardized setup can help you scale effortlessly when growth comes.

◆ These case studies are proof that IT can be a liability or a superpower, depending on how you handle it.

The stories are real, and the lessons are clear. But now it's your move.

In the final chapter, I'll help you take stock, take action, and find the support you need to keep building a business that works smarter and stays ready.

You're Not Alone: Next Steps and Support

What's Next?

If you've made it this far — first off, kudos! You've stuck with a tech book written not for engineers or IT departments but for real-world business owners who are just trying to get this stuff *right*.

You don't need to be a tech expert. You just need to know enough to make smart decisions, delegate wisely, and hold your vendors accountable. And now? You do.

This final chapter is all about **what to do next** and how to get help if you need it.

Step 1: Do a Quick IT Self-Check

Take 20 minutes. Grab a coffee. And, instead of guessing where you stand, head over to this quick, practical IT self-assessment survey I put together for businesses like yours: bhtechconnection.com/it-action-plan.

This free tool walks you through many of the key areas we've covered in this book (backup strategy, email platform, security habits, and more to be expanded over time). It'll give you a clear picture of your current IT posture and help you identify the right next move.

Once you know where the gaps are, you can fill them confidently without wasting time on the wrong stuff.

Step 2. Pick One Area to Improve

IT doesn't have to be all or nothing. Start where the pain is most visible or the risk is highest:

◆ No password manager? Start there.

◆ Still using a personal Gmail for client work? Time to move.

◆ No backup solution? Fix that before anything else.

Small changes here *really do* make a big difference.

Step 3. Build or Find Your Support System

You're not in this alone. Whether it's a local IT partner, a part-time, tech-savvy VA, or a fractional vCIO who helps set your roadmap, **you don't have to wear every hat forever**.

Here's what good support looks like:

◆ They understand your business size and industry.

◆ They can speak human, not just tech.

CHAPTER 18. YOU'RE NOT ALONE:
NEXT STEPS AND SUPPORT

- They'll train your staff and empower you to ask questions.
- They document what they do and share it with you.

The right IT partner will make you feel in control, not confused or dependent.

This Book Is Just the Beginning

You've now got the foundational knowledge that most business owners wish they had years ago. The next step? Use it.

Whether you:

- Audit your current tools.
- Bring in a vendor for help.
- Start budgeting for IT support.
- Forward this book to your business partner and say, "Read this!"

The TL;DR

- You don't have to be an IT expert, but you can't ignore IT either.
- Start with an honest self-assessment.
- Fix one thing at a time. Small wins stack up.
- Build a support system that scales with you.
- You've got this. You're not alone.

APPENDIX A

References List

Chapter 1

1. Hava. *2024 Cloud Market Share Analysis: Decoding Industry Leaders and Trends.* Retrieved April 12, 2025, from https://www.hava.io/blog/2024-cloud-market-share-analysis-decoding-industry-leaders-and-trends

2. https://www.redhotcyber.com/en/post/businesses-are-going-bankrupt-due-to-ransomware-small-and-medium-sized-businesses-beware/#:~:text=It%20is%20precisely%20these%20companies,months%20after%20a%20cyber%20attack

3. Atlassian. *The True Cost of Downtime.* Retrieved April 12, 2025, from https://www.atlassian.com/incident-management/kpis/cost-of-downtime#:~:text=The%20average%20cost%20of%20downtime&text=And%20since%202014%2C%20that%20figure,$137%20to%20$427%20per%20minute

Chapter 2

4. CISA. *Shields Up Guidance for Families.* Retrieved April 12, 2025, from https://www.cisa.gov/shields-guidance-families

5. Verisign. *4 Myths About Using a Branded Email for Business.* Retrieved April 12, 2025, from https://blog.verisign.com/getting-online/4-myths-about-using-a-branded-email-for-business/

Chapter 3

6. Enterprise Apps Today. *Backup Statistics.* Retrieved April 12, 2025, from https://www.enterpriseappstoday.com/stats/backup-statistics.html

7. PRWeb. *New Study Reveals One in Three SMBs Use Free Consumer Cybersecurity and One in Five Use No Endpoint Security at All.* Retrieved April 12, 2025, from https://www.prweb.com/releases/new-study-reveals-one-in-three-smbs-use-free-consumer-cybersecurity-and-one-in-five-use-no-endpoint-security-at-all-824695692.html

8. Unitrends. *What Are the Consequences of Data Loss?* Retrieved April 12, 2025, from https://www.unitrends.com/blog/what-are-the-consequences-of-data-loss/#:~:text=The%20consequences%20of%20data%20loss%20are%20dire;,bankruptcy%20within%20one%20year%20of%20the%20disaster

Chapter 4

9. US Small Business Administration. *Cyber Safety Tips for Small Business Owners.* Retrieved April 12, 2025, from https://www.sba.gov/blog/2023/2023-09/cyber-safety-tips-small-business-owners

10. Aligned Insurance Agency. *The True Cost of Cyberattacks on Small Businesses.* Retrieved April 12, 2025, from https://alignedinsuranceagency.com/posts-general-liability/the-true-cost-of-cyberattacks-on-small-businesses-what-every-business-owner-needs-to-know/

11. U.S. Small Business Administration. *Cyber Safety Tips for Small Business Owners.* Retrieved April 12, 2025, from https://www.sba.gov/blog/2023/2023-09/cyber-safety-tips-small-business-owners

Chapter 6

12. JumpCloud. *Multi-Factor Authentication Statistics: 2023 Trends and Insights.* Retrieved April 12, 2025, from https://jumpcloud.com/blog/multi-factor-authentication-statistics

13. LastPass. *The Current State of SMB Password Management.* Retrieved April 12, 2025, from https://blog.lastpass.com/posts/the-current-state-of-smb-password-management

Chapter 7

14. CyLab at Carnegie Mellon University. *Workplace Password Sharing Study.* Retrieved April 12, 2025, from https://www.cylab.cmu.edu/news/2019/11/22-shared-accounts-workplace.html

15. Beyond Identity. *Ex-Employee Access Risk Statistics.* Retrieved April 12, 2025, from https://www.beyondidentity.com/resource/former-employees-admit-to-using-continued-account-access-to-harm-previous-employers

Chapter 8

16. Smartsheet. *Workers Waste a Quarter of the Work Week on Manual, Repetitive Tasks.* Retrieved April 12, 2025, from https://www.smartsheet.com/content-center/product-news/automation/workers-waste-quarter-work-week-manual-repetitive-tasks#:~:text=Workers%20believe%20that%20automating%20these,be%20automated%20(59%20percent)

17. McKinsey & Company. *The Imperatives for Automation Success.* Retrieved April 12, 2025, from https://www.mckinsey.com/~/media/McKinsey/Business%20Functions/Operations/Our%20Insights/The%20imperatives%20for%20automation%20success/The-imperatives-for-automation-success.pdf

18. https://xkcd.com/1205/

Chapter 9

19. Zylo. *SaaS Management Index 2023*. Retrieved April 12, 2025, from https://zylo.com/blog/manage-saas-licenses-with-usage-insights/

Chapter 10

20. TechRepublic. *Disaster Recovery Testing Practices Among SMBs*. Retrieved April 12, 2025, from https://www.techrepublic.com/article/why-23-of-companies-never-test-their-disaster-recovery-plan-despite-major-risks/

21. Veeam. *2023 Ransomware Trends Report*. Retrieved April 12, 2025, from https://www.veeam.com/ransomware-trends-report-2023

Chapter 11

22. Acronis. *Cyber Protection Week Global Report 2022*. Retrieved April 12, 2025, from https://dl.acronis.com/u/rc/Acronis-Cyber-Protection-Week-Global-Report-2022.pdf

Chapter 12

23. BusinessWire. *Global Managed Services Market 2022-2027: Big Data Stands to Be Driving Factor for Productivity and Efficiency*. Retrieved April 12, 2025, from https://www.businesswire.com/news/home/20220218005441/en/Global-Managed-Services-Market-2022---2027-Big-Data-Stands-to-be-Driving-Factor-for-Productivity-and-Efficiency---ResearchAndMarkets.com

Chapter 13

24. Entrepreneur. *How Small Businesses Are Adopting Digital Tools to Manage Growth*. Retrieved April 12, 2025, from https://www.entrepreneur.com/growing-a-business/over-half-of-small-businesses-are-struggling-to-grow/482623

25. The Sun. *Lack of Technical Knowledge Is Holding Back Nearly Half of UK Small Businesses.* Retrieved April 12, 2025, from https://www.thesun.co.uk/money/22535838/lack-technical-knowledge-small-businesses-paypal/

Chapter 14

26. McKinsey & Company. *Americans Are Embracing Flexible Work - and They Want More of It.* Retrieved April 12, 2025, from https://www.mckinsey.com/industries/real-estate/our-insights/americans-are-embracing-flexible-work-and-they-want-more-of-it

27. Appical. *Employee Onboarding Statistics.* Retrieved April 12, 2025, from https://www.appical.com/resources/blog/employee-onboarding-statistics?utm_source=chatgpt.com

Chapter 15

28. SHRM. *HR Outsourcing and Small Business Risk.* Retrieved April 12, 2025, from https://www.shrm.org/topics-tools/news/organizational-employee-development/small-business-hr

Chapter 16

29. MedPage Today. *How Much Could a Data Breach Cost Your Practice?* Retrieved April 12, 2025, from https://www.medpagetoday.com/resource-centers/osteoporosis/much-data-breach-cost-your-practice/715#:~:text=Each%20HIPAA%20violation%20can%20cost,lawsuits%20and%20the%20associated%20expenses

Starter Kit and Core Stack Guide

Whether you're a team of one or a fast-growing crew, this Starter Kit gives you a simple, trustworthy foundation to build from. These aren't theoretical recommendations. They're the same tools I've helped hundreds of businesses implement, customized for the realities of working in professional services with limited time and budget.

The Core Stack (Essentials for Every Size Business)

Domain Registration and Website

- **Domain registrar:** Stick with reliable registrars like GoDaddy or Namecheap. But **never use them** for email or website hosting. Buy your domain here, and nothing else.

- **Email hosting:** Always use your chosen productivity suite (Google Workspace or Microsoft 365) for email. Do *not* host email through your domain registrar!

- **Website platform:** If you need a professional-looking site with flexibility and SEO performance, WordPress (hosted with providers like WP Engine or SiteGround) is the way to go. Avoid Wix, Squarespace, or anything bundled with your registrar. They're fine for placeholders but not serious business infrastructure.

- ◆ **Note:** While there are some legal battles between WordPress and WP Engine, as of this writing it doesn't mean WP Engine isn't still a major provider of hosting services for WordPress-built websites.

Hardware Buying Guide: Minimum Recommended Specs (as of 2025)

Processor

- ◆ Minimum specs: Intel i5 (11th Gen or newer) / AMD Ryzen 5 / Apple M1+
- ◆ Notes: i7 or Ryzen 7/M2+ if multitasking or heavier workloads (engineering, coding)

RAM

- ◆ Minimum specs: 16GB
- ◆ Notes: 8GB is not enough, especially with browser-heavy workflows

Storage

- • Minimum specs: 512GB SSD (NVMe preferred)
- • Notes: SSD is a must. Avoid HDDs. Upgrade to 1TB if you store local files.

OS

- ◆ Minimum specs: Windows 11 Pro, macOS Ventura+
- ◆ Notes: Avoid Home editions. Pro adds admin tools and security features.

These specs ensure you're not bottlenecking productivity, even as your business grows. Spending a little more now will save you from early obsolescence or replacement.

- **Laptops:** Look for business-grade devices (not consumer models). Dell Latitude, Lenovo ThinkPad, and HP ProBook lines are great options. Do you want to be a Mac shop? Then commit to that for everyone at the company. Standardization is key. Avoid Chromebooks unless you're in an entirely cloud-based workflow and don't need any local software.

- **Routers/networking:** Use a router that supports WPA3 and ideally has some form of built-in threat detection or firewall capabilities. Ubiquiti, ASUS, or Netgear's business lines are solid choices. If you don't have a centralized office and everyone works out of their homes, you can probably skip this bit.

- **Accessories:** Docking stations, webcams, and noise-canceling headsets make a big difference in productivity, especially for remote work or hybrid environments.

Core Stack Comparison: Google Workspace vs. Microsoft 365

Google Workspace

- Advantages: Collaboration, Gmail, simplicity
- Email hosting: Gmail-based
- File storage: Google Drive + Shared Drives
- Admin control: Very good
- HIPAA/FINRA support: HIPAA (with BAA)
- Backup compatibility: Spanning, Backupify

Microsoft 365

- ◆ Advantages: Outlook users, Excel, compliance
- ◆ Email hosting: Outlook-based
- ◆ File storage: OneDrive + SharePoint
- ◆ Admin control: Excellent (especially with Azure AD)
- ◆ HIPAA/FINRA support: Yes (stronger compliance tools)
- ◆ Backup compatibility: Spanning, Dropsuite, Veeam

Password Management

- ◆ **LastPass for Business**, **1Password**, or **Dashlane for Business**: Pick one, roll it out org-wide, and enforce it.

Backup and Recovery

- ◆ **Spanning by Kaseya:** Covers Google Workspace or Microsoft 365 data (email, Google Drive/OneDrive, calendars)

Cyber Liability Insurance

- ◆ **Datastream insurance:** A good starting point for realistic small-business coverage. But be sure to do your due diligence!

Tools by Industry

Legal Firms

- ◆ **Clio:** End-to-end law practice management (time tracking, document storage, client communications)

Financial Services

- **Redtail:** FINRA-compliant CRM, purpose-built for financial advisors

Tools by Company Size

Solo Operators

- Google Workspace or Microsoft 365
- MFA enabled on all devices and logins
- Password manager (no spreadsheets!)
- Basic backups
- Scheduling tools (Calendly, Microsoft Bookings)

Small Teams (2-5)

- Start with some simple CRMs (HubSpot Free, CapsuleCRM).
- Add Shared Drives/SharePoint Sites.
- Standardize folder structure and naming conventions.
- Create an onboarding/offboarding checklist, both for HR and IT elements.
- Acquire cyber insurance + tested backups.
- Create role-based access across all systems.

Growing Teams (6-20)

- Documented IT policies
- Dedicated network equipment and/or zero-trust tools (ThreatLocker)

Setup Priorities

Day 1 Must-Haves

◆ Domain name

◆ Business-grade email platform

◆ MFA + password manager

◆ Backup for core platforms

Next 30 Days

◆ Build a website.

◆ Standardize file structure.

◆ Set up shared calendars and drives.

◆ Create an onboarding checklist.

Long-Term Planning

◆ Cyber insurance

◆ Security awareness training

◆ Strategic IT planning (vCIO, if possible)

Resources

Free Resources

- NIST cybersecurity overview: https://www.nist.gov/cybersecurity
- NIST Cybersecurity Framework 2.0: Small Business: https://doi.org/10.6028/NIST.SP.1300
- NIST Risk Management Framework Small Enterprise: https://doi.org/10.6028/NIST.SP.1314
- Guide for Employers: https://www.ftc.gov/system/files/attachments/cybersecurity-small-business/cybersecurity_sb_discussion-guide_101218.pdf

Stay Current: Key Regulatory Resources

Regulations evolve constantly. Staying compliant means keeping a finger on the pulse of the latest updates. Bookmark the following authoritative pages that apply to your business and make it a regular practice to check them periodically:

- HIPAA compliance: U.S. Department of Health & Human Services, https://www.hhs.gov/hipaa

- ◆ FINRA compliance: FINRA, https://www.finra.org/rules-guidance
- ◆ SEC regulations: U.S. Securities and Exchange Commission, https://www.sec.gov/regulation

Regularly revisiting these sites will ensure your business remains informed, compliant, and ready to adapt swiftly to any regulatory changes.

www.ingramcontent.com/pod-product-compliance
Lightning Source LLC
Chambersburg PA
CBHW071544200326
41519CB00021BB/6608